I have sold this copy to you at a Bargain price — at a loss, but Money is not every thing! Think Kindly of me — [illegible] you ever know any [illegible] reliable speaker [illegible] any kind of club mention ME I'll be happy to come & talk — if only to get away from my very Lonely Life — & to meet folks & perhaps make a new friend!

Sincerely

Fred Bason

D1179862

THE LAST BASSOON

Fred Bason has also written

Bibliography of the Writings of W. Somerset Maugham
Gallery Unreserved (*Introduction by W. Somerset Maugham*)
The Cigarette Card Collector's Handbook
Toys for Nothing
More Toys for Nothing
Fred Bason's First Diary (*edited by Nicolas Bentley*)
The Second Diary of Fred Bason (*edited by L. A. G. Strong*)
Fred Bason's Third Diary (*edited by Michael Sadleir*)
Fishing
Contributions to Volumes V to XX of The Saturday Book
etc.

THE LAST BASSOON

from the diaries of

FRED BASON

Edited and Introduced by

NOËL COWARD

MAX PARRISH · LONDON

MAX PARRISH AND CO LTD
55 QUEEN ANNE STREET
LONDON W1

To the ten thousand friends
I have made via my former diaries
(and that, I hope, includes you)

© FRED BASON 1960
PRINTED IN GREAT BRITAIN BY
EAST MIDLAND PRINTING COMPANY LIMITED
BURY ST EDMUNDS, PETERBOROUGH, KETTERING
AND ELSEWHERE

Foreword

After having read Fred Bason's first three diaries, I have edited his fourth, and, in case the *aficionado* is worried lest his English might have improved, I hasten to report that the Cockney is as full-flavoured as ever. Indeed, like Maurice Chevalier's English accent, I believe it has ripened with the years. Where would Mr Bason be without his Gorblimeys and where would Monsieur Chevalier be without those r's rippling and gurgling ever deeper in the throat ?

Those awful contingencies, however, need not worry us ; it is extremely unlikely that they will ever arise. Maurice, of course, would be a great artist whatever his accent, and nothing on earth would stop Fred Bason from being a writer. He scribbles or writes or types his remarks and reflections on any subject, old or new, that comes to mind, and on any old, or new, bit of paper that comes to hand. Out of all his many activities, I suspect that he gets his deepest pleasure from writing. When the blinds are drawn in his house at the end of the day, the latest autographs – Rosamond Lehmann's or Doris Day's or Lord Morrison's – put in their place, and cigarette card No. 19 of the series has come at last to rest between 18 and 20, then, like the Brontës after Papa had gone to bed, the pen races over the paper.

Editing such a mass of material has not been easy, and I may have, not unnaturally, inclined more to the theatrical entries than for instance those from the world of boxing, but there is something here for everyone, and many glimpses into a side of life in London from the Twenties to the Fifties that no one else can give us.

Some of the entries have already appeared in *The Saturday Book*, and the editor's courtesy in allowing the use of these is acknowledged.

NOËL COWARD
1960

By Way of Explanation

I have been faithfully keeping a day to day diary for more than thirty years. I was advised to do this by the late James Agate who said that if I would keep a diary that diary may some day keep me. The only thing its keepted me is HAPPY. . .and thats something. This is the fourth and the last portion of my diary and for that reason I have called it *The Last Bassoon.* The title comes from a part of The Ancient Mariner and Agate suggested that title when I thought Id had enough of being a diarist. Well, Ive had enough. Ive had a very long run for my so called literary career, and although I shall probably write other books I dont expect to ever compile another diary.

I will tell you why. Firstly, I am alone in this world. I have no wife, no sweetheart and I dont seem to have any relations left. I have no one but a very faithful landlady. I do have some friends (Thank God) and I wish to keep them. But the trouble with being a diarist is that one half of your friends want to be in your diaries and the other half *fear* to be in them ! When you put them in they dont like what youve written about them, and if you leave them out they are annoyed ! You are invited to a party and notice folks fear to speak to you, in case you put them into a diary. You have to get up and assure everyone on your honour that its a NIGHT OFF, and *nothing* will be used.

I wouldn't knowingly annoy anyone. There is less than eight stone of me and I am not of the stuff that heroes are made from. I like peace and quiet and my friends are extreemly precious to me. Besides, a man cannot keep on diarying. James Agate, who in my opinion was the best of modern diarists, finished his Ego's when he was very very feeble and in great pain. I want to finish my Cockney diaries when I am ever so well and have not a cloud in my sky.

Diary one was edited by Nicolas Bentley. It made two editions and sold over ten thousand copies. Diary two was edited by L. A. G. Strong. It had praise from 162 newspapers and did well. My third diary had an introduction and was edited by Michael Sadleir. And now, now I finish on a *cressendo* – Introduced and edited by Noël Coward ! I believe that this book is the very first in all his career he has both introduced and edited, and he did it for NOTHING – for nothing but sheer goodwill. Its worth recording the fact that the first book I wrote had an introduction by W. Somerset Maugham (1931).

Yes, Ive had a very good run for my time and trouble and no regrets for ever becoming a writer of sorts. Oh, I am very conscious of my limitations, but this can be said for my writings : Ive never failed to amuse and surely that is really something in these days !

I know that Noël Coward got much amusement as he sorted out my bits and pieces. I hope that you will get pleasure from reading the finished work. I was never cut out to be a literary gent. This is my final bow as a Cockney diariest.

FRED BASON
1960

1920. The Outing. A memory of when I was thirteen

Life to children is a thing consisting of moments and because of this unhappy fact there are many links missing from the chain in retrospect, moments which were small, rather dim, and seemly of little importance. It is the big moments of our childhood that we are able to recall to mind easily. It is given to few of us to vividly remember our childhood (or youth) that is why a deal of nonsense is often written about childhood. For my part, I remember a very unhappy childhood with a mother and father who were both over forty when I was unexpectedly born. I remember quite often being told that I was unwanted. But even in my unhappy childhood days there were moments of happiness and a big one stands out clearly in my memory. It happened when I was thirteen.

My grandfather was a very religious man, and a good man at that. He lived in the days I am writing about, in a street just behind Walworth Road Baptist Chapel, about half a mile from my home. I did not visit him often, because he always insisted that he and I knelt down and then said a very long prayer all about my sins, and leading me into the paths of righteousness. I always felt very uneasy in his presence, although I say again he was a very good man and he meant well.

On the corner of Vowler Street where he lived, there was a rather high-class provision store, a regular little gold mine of a one-man business. I knew it was a gold mine because the owner of it always smoked Manikin cigars and wore a heavy gold watch chain, with a gold watch on the end of it! This grocer had one child, a girl named Gertie, who was his pride and joy. Nothing was too good for Gertie. Even I, with an almost complete lack of worldly wisdom of females could see that she was a cut above the average girls of Walworth, for she wore a special school uniform and on her neat hat was a school crest.

Gertie was a special friend of mine, and I was mighty proud of her friendship. Yes, she was my 'sweetie'. The more I got to know her the more frequently I visited my grandfather, because on my way to his home I passed the grocer's shop and could see Gertie. My mother never knew that my special girl friend was the real reason why I called on my grandfather ! If my mother knew that meeting Gertie gave me great delight, she would have forbidden it, just out of sheer cussidness, she was like that.

Now, Gertie had a hobby – the collecting of cigarette cards – and we spent many happy moments outside her dad's shop, exchanging cards. She liked cards with flowers on them, I liked soldiers. We happily swopped our finds to our mutual satisfaction. We also played a game called 'closest to the Wall', in which we flicked cigarette cards in turn towards a wall, and the one whose card fell closest in turn towards that wall, took the other one's card. I often won back from her all the cards that I had swopped with her, because I was pretty good at this game. The reason why I was nearly an expert, was that I used to lick the edge of the card and press my fingers hard against the wet edge of the pasteboard, until it became stiffened, then it would fly faster and I could control its flight better – and it usually fell just where I wanted it to fall. Gertie would never lick, she said it was neither healthy or lady-like. My sweetie was extremely kind to me. My parents were poor, and I was very often hungry. I was a slim whippersnapper of a Cockney. Gertie knew a great deal about food, loved food, and in consequence was lovely and plump, and I liked plump ladies then – and I do now. She was cuddly, but I had never dared to attempt to cuddle her ! Looking back, I am very sure that Gertie was my first love and I loved her more each time that she ran into her dad's shop and came out with a tasty bit of this or that for me – which she called 'a sampler'. One day, I remember Gertie giving me a very tasty creamy rich French pastry. It was the first French pastry I had ever eaten. It made me sick and bilious, and I had to explain to her that I was not used to such rich things. But I learned a few days after this event, through one of her friends, that Gertie wanted to give me the best of everything, as she had a real crush on little me ! That bit of news made up for the biliousness. We didn't kiss. We didn't hold hands – people might see – but being together for even a little while was happiness. Looking back, I don't know if I was spellbound by the charm of Gertie, or the delights of the food she gave me !

One day she invited me to go with her on a picnic. 'We will take our bikes,' she said, 'and go up to Peckham Rye and have a lovely picnic.' I told her that I was not able to provide any food. 'Food,' she said, 'I will get all that. You leave that to me. Hasn't my daddy got a shopfull of food ? He will give me anything I want. Leave it to me, dear Freddy.'

We arranged to meet at Camberwell Green on the following Saturday afternoon. For five days and nights I dreamed of that forthcoming picnic, the first one of my humble life. I didn't call on Gertie in the meantime. I suppose I realised that absence makes the heart grow fonder, and I wanted that fondness to be on both sides, as we had a real lovely picnic, food and other nice things. I thought of her, and all the nice food she would bring, by day and by night. On the Saturday, I made myself as respectable-looking as I was able, even to the extent of polishing my shoes and combing my hair twice. I polished the chromium handlebars on my very ancient bicycle. Gertie's bike was a very expensive model, in brilliant blue enamel and with gears and a huge bell. I didn't want to disgrace her. My bike had been painted black with tar, which came off on my hands every time I touched it. But this Saturday, at any rate, I made the handlebars sparkle.

Then I sat down to my dinner, which I recall, consisted of a thick slice of bread with dripping on it and a cup of horrible cocoa – I never liked cocoa – and my mother knew this, but she always insisted on cocoa for Saturday. This time I drank the cocoa and didn't really mind. Wasn't I going to have a marvellous picnic ? As I sipped that hot cocoa my mind flitted over the lovely possibilities of the afternoon. It just couldn't fail to be a really lovely turnout. Maybe she'd even bring strawberries and real cream. I knew her Dad stocked both in his shop. I had never had strawberries and cream, but I knew they were luxuries. My, what a real tuck in we would have !

I got to Camberwell Green a quarter of an hour before the appointed time, and there I sat on my bike watching the traffic go by. It was a perfect day. I was at peace with the world, with not a cloud on my horizon.

Gertie arrived right on the tick of time. I said 'Hello.' Just that. She said 'Hello,' just that. And off we pedalled down the Peckham Road, towards Peckham Rye, the largest open space in our slum part of London. I noted that my girl friend had a box and a blanket on the carrier at the back of her bike. This excited me, and I set up a pretty smart pace as we cycled along. Gertie kept up with me the whole way : I was quite proud of her.

When we got to the Rye, Gertie suggested that we should walk up a small hill to some distant trees and sit under them. But they seemed to me to be a long way off, and I was both tired and hungry. So I pointed out to Gertie that things are likely to drop on you when you sit under trees, and that we didn't want anything to spoil our picnic. 'Very well,' she said, so I quickly untied the basket and the blanket from the back of her bike.

As I spread the blanket out on the soft grass, Gertie stood and watched me, with a smile on her pretty face. I spread the blanket out very neatly, and then placed the basket of good things in the exact centre, sat down on the edge of the blanket and waited for my girl to be hostess. She sat down very close to me, and for a brief moment she held my hand. Her face was close to mine, and she smelt lovely. I very nearly kissed her. Very nearly – but not quite – people might see. Up to the age of thirteen, I don't think I had given more than five kisses to girls in my young life, and even then with extreme shyness. I knew she wanted to be kissed, one does, but let's face it, I'd come for a picnic, and kissing girls was considered most unmanly in my part of London.

After a while, she began to open the picnic basket. This was the Great Moment – the moment I'd dreamed about for five days and nights. What would it be – lemonade ? Lovely cream pastries ? Thick sausage rolls ? Rich meaty ham ? Strawberries and cream ? Or something so luxurious that I had never heard of it ? My mouth watered with anticipation.

She lifted the lid and turned back the paper wrappings. I gasped. In the box were two bread rolls, two small pieces of not very nice looking cheese, two apples and a lemonade bottle, containing milk ! There were also two paper napkins with forget-me-nots at the corners. Trust Gertie to bring napkins – she was always a lady ! I could easily have cried with disappointment. So this – this was what I'd been dreaming of. Bleeding bread and cheese – and MILK ! Blooming milk – did she think as how I was an infant ? Milk ! It was a cruel shame. I felt real angry. For a moment, I felt like smacking her face. She must have seen the mixed expressions in my face. She said, 'I was going to bring such nice things really I was. Crab and a tin of pineapple and lots of jam tarts and things like that, but my dad said that you were probably used to plain food and that rich things would not agree with you. And I was afraid to make you bilious, like you were when you had that French pastry. And mummy said something plain would be much better for a growing boy.' A growing boy ! Something PLAIN ! She was hurling insults after injury. I could hardly speak. I didn't know what to say – I realised it was not her fault.

'Oh well, don't talk so much,' I said, 'let's get on with it.' So we got on with it. The roll was crusty and hard, the cheese tasted like soap. The apple had a maggot in it. I managed to swallow my pride and take a small sip of milk. I ask you – what Walworth man would be seen drinking milk ? And with a girl at that. It was a most shameful position to be in, and I was grateful that no other boys from Walworth were on that Rye. I would never have been able to have lived it down. Soon it was over.

'Don't you like our picnic, Freddy ?'

I didn't answer, I got up, found a large stone and threw it at a little dog that was sniffing round. As the dog ran away, I ran after it, just for something to do. I didn't want to say I hated the picnic, and that it had been a very great disappointment to me. I didn't want to offend her, only really, she ought to have known better. Dash it all, she lived in Walworth, and was one year older than me. She ought to have used her loaf. I must have been away just five minutes, chasing that dog, and when I got back she was crying ! Well, blimey, that capped everything.

'Cor, luv a duck,' I said, 'do put a sock in it.'

But I suppose that she was enjoying herself in her own silly way for she didn't stop crying. So again I went for a walk, this time to several good belches, because I now had indigestion from the dry roll and hard cheese. I remembered my mother saying, more than once, never make wind in the presence of a lady – and Gertie was a lady.

When I got back to Gertie she had ceased to cry. The

skies looked overcast, and as if they were going to start weeping at any moment. While I was tying the blanket onto the carrier of my girl's bike, it began to rain. She had, of course, a rainproof cycling cape, which I undid and handed to her. I had no mac or protection at all from the rain. I kicked the picnic box away and chucked the milk cum-lemonade bottle into a bush. Then I told Gertie to get on her bike and let us start for home. Just as I was getting on my bike, I noted one of the forget-me-not napkins on the grass, so I picked it up and put it into my pocket.

On the way home, I got absolutely soaked with rain from head to foot. Although I peddled at a furious rate, she kept up with me. We were at the top of my road. I said 'Goodbye', just that. She said 'goodbye' – just that. I could not bring myself to thank her for the lovely picnic ! When I got home, I was in proper trouble, for getting wet, and I had to explain just where I'd been. Picnic ! On an outing ! I'll give you outing ! You'll go to your room and stay in. Outing indeed ! Go upstairs and change everything. And stay there. No tea for you. Getting yourself all wet. You'll be ill and then expect me to get you well again. You are a cruel thoughtless boy !

So up I went to my cold and bleak attic. And there I had a blooming good cry, as I changed my clothes and made myself dry again.

It was all of six weeks before I again went to see my granddad, and to pass Gertie's home. As I passed the shop, I looked into the window to see what lovely grub they had on display and to try to see Gertie, and beckon her out for a chat with me. I wanted to explain. To tell her I was sorry. I had not been very polite. It had not been her fault, she had meant so well. In the middle of the window was a big notice in flaming red which said UNDER NEW MANAGEMENT, BUT STILL THE SAME HIGH CLASS STANDARD. I knew what Under New Management meant. I plucked up my courage and went inside. The new shopkeeper was not a bit like Gertie's Dad. He had no watch chain. I enquired what had happened to the former owner, and was told that he had had a stroke and the whole family had moved away and retired from business.

'Can I serve you with anything, my little man ?' said the new proprietor. I said 'No thanks'. And in my secret mind I said that he would never ever serve me with anything – fancy calling me a little man – that was a dead liberty. Little man indeed – who did he think he was ?

I never ever saw Gertie again. I often wondered what became of her. Right up to the blitz I kept that paper napkin with the forget-me-nots in the corners as a reminder of my very first outing. I hope Gertie found happiness in life, and that as the years went on, her own children had picnics, and not with maggots in their apples. It was the maggot in the apple that kept this event more in my mind than anything else. As I said at the beginning, life for children is a thing of moments, and this outing was a big moment in my young life. How could I ever forget it ?

(The above piece appeared many years ago in *The Saturday Book*. Long after it was published, a lady wrote in to John Hadfield, the editor, and said she had read a similar story in a book (title forgotten) by Julius Wechsberg. Well, I'm sorry, but I've told it exactly as it happened to Gertie and me, and the shop is still there on the corner of Vowler Street. Seems that J. Wechsberg and me are just two of the thousands of men who have been deceived by a woman.)

1921

This is a very happy day. From Roma, Via della Purificazione 8, wherever that happens to be, a great music master has kept a promise to me. V. de Pachmann has at last sent me his autograph. When I asked him personally he gave a funny little dance, a tiny whistle and a NO. Then he said

Address please, so I gave him a used envelope. He took it and then raised his fragile hands to heaven and sighed. Then he got into a huge car. Why do little men always have big cars ? To make them look smaller ? Well, after six months silence Pachmann has obliged me. He was such a nice little man. Funny little man. He was taught playing piano by Chopin, and is first bloke Ive ever seen who really looks a musician. And he wouldn't have looked a bit like that if he had had a haircut.

1922

There is a word which I cant spell which is used by 'posh' people when they look back on the past. I dont think that it is meditation but it is something like that. I am going to look back, my diary, at last year.

One thing stands out proper well. I remember more than anything else the hiding, the beating that poor Georges Carpentier got from Jack Dempsey. It might seem proper silly for me what is very English to think so very much about a Frenchman who I have only met twice, and about an American tough who I aint *ever* seen in person, but its a fact that I was really down right upset when Carpentier was defeated.

And it was NOT that I lost two shillings on the result that upset me. In the barber shop where I work (its in Albany Road, Camberwell) its betting all the day. I bet on a couple of flies crawling up the window. I bet on the turn of a card. I like a bet. My father has been betting on the race horses all of his life. He aint never won much. He loses far more often than he wins, but if he didnt have his daily bet he would have very little in life to live for. He is a harness maker, a saddler, and amongst horses every day. Its natural-like that he should bet on the things that earn him his living. But I dont like horses. I like people. I bet mostly on men, or on the turn of a card. Barbers and their assistants get a lot of so called from the horses mouth information. Its aint *really* information – its just fairly good guessing, but you have to listen to customers and you *have* to show an interest in their selections.

I pass the information on to my dad and to other customers. If they are lucky in their wins, I get what is called a 'slice from their cake' – a bit of commission. I put this in a box under the floorboards under my bed so that my mother dont ever get her hands on it. When I need some for books and things I goes to it. Books are my best pleasure. I like a good read. I like W. W. Jacobs and Arnold Bennett. I like Zane Grey, R. L. Stevenson and Conan Doyle. Mr Zane Grey has sent me a nice photograph of himself from America. I wrote to him care of Hodders and I cant really say that I expected any answer. Blessed is them what don't expect . . . I got !

I like ever so much going to the pictures, but its not often I can see all of a picture show. I works long hours. 1921 was unhappy at home. I do wish I had a brother or a sister. Well, I have now looked back. This year ought to be better for me.

Friday, 25th August, 1922

In four days time I will be fifteen. I am still in a barbers shop, and I hate it. I dont get home untill nearly 8.30 except on Thursdays when we close at one. I then have to tidy up the shop, and its two before I am allowed to leave. I have written to the local paper, and I know its impudent of me. I have written to tell them to put cheerful news on the front page of their paper and leave all the suicides and tragadies and deaths to page seven and eight. I have not had a reply. I dont think they will reply, but if they will only change the style then I will feel I have done a bit of real good.

On Sunday we are going to see Southwark Bridge. My diary, why do I record this event ? Nothing in going to see a bridge. But this is the newest bridge over the Thames and has been opened just ONE year. It cost 360,000 pounds to build. And now its going to be, or is now being, *torn up* entirely in order to lay down electric cables and other things. I do not understand why they didnt put down the cables and other things when they were BUILDING the bridge. . . and not destroy a perfectly new bridge at a further cost of over ten thousand pounds. But we are going to see it on Sunday in case it gets all pulled down to rebuild the bridge. Coming shortly at local cinemas are John Barrymore in *Jekyll and Hyde* and M. Lang in *Mr Wu*. BOTH are very sad. Sam Mayo is coming to the local music hall, and he is very sad as well ! I dont see anything funny coming our way, and so Dad and me is going to see a perfectly new bridge pulled up – and that should be FUNNY.

On my Birthday, August 29th, 1922. I am 15

I don't suppose that it will ever matter to anyone to know that *before* I was eleven years old I had read (and in many cases re-read) every word of every page of the following Books :

Swiss Family Robinson
Robinson Crusoe
Treasure Island
Adventures of Sherlock Holmes
King Solomon Mines
Vanity Fair
The Adventures of Tom Sawyer.

I did *not* like Tom Sawyer or Vanity Fair. I read Swiss Family Robinson *nine* times.

But my treasure, the Book I valued *most* of all, was Pear's Cyclopaedia. From the age of 10 till at least 14 it was my *Constant companion*. Now I have a Brainfull of almost *useless* facts that won't bring me in a penny, a mis-cellous collection of oddments and no *real knowledge of Anything at all* ! I am a larther boy and I hate it. I want to become a seller of books. I love books. I hate dirty mens dirty chins. Their beards are like sandpaper. My poor hands are sore with larthering them. What a blooming life. Gor Blimey !

1922

Stacy Aumonier isn't a poet but he looks like one. He has a rather mournfull face and sad eyes. There isn't a more modest bloke writing to day – and his short stories are quite jewels. I've met Mr Aumonier. He's given me a luncheon – and I've given him two Books he was 'dying to get'. So I've stopped him dying and the world owes me something for that. Stacy told me a good tale. Once at a Theatre the audience was very inattentive and nothing said on the stage could be heard for the din of chatter made by the audience. The leading man became angry and going to the footlights he said 'Unless this play is *stopped you cannot go on talking* !' There was a moral somewhere in that tale. I couldn't think *what*.

12th September 1922

On this wonderfull day at Swan and Edgars a glorious fairy named Aileen Stanley, who is a great Vaudeville singer, spent twelve pounds on me to make me look a perfect little English gent. She said I was a perfect gentleman to speak to and the politest Englishman she'd met. I was also the only autograph collector who had remembered to say Thank you. Now out of kindness of heart she has bought me clothes to make me look a gent as well. Oh I am so very happy. Ive never had such luck before. I am wearing all the lovely rig out now and I am to go to The Palladium tonight to show her how I look. Another wonderfull thing. I have left barbaring forever. A docter said the atmosphere was killing me. But if anything I now have a bleedin sight worst job. I am at the wrong end of a planing machine, pulling out planks of wood as they are planed. The machine spreads out chips and sawdust like blooming fury and there's me covered all the day, and the noise is awfull. When can I become me own master ? I hope ever so soon, soon as I get enough capital for stock. My dad got me this job in the carpentry place. He would !

29th October 1922

Yesterday at The Ring in Blackfriars Road I had a very nice conversation with Ted Broadribb, the boxing manager. He lives in Walworth, not far from me. He is probally most famous bloke in my district. We talked boxing pretty near 15 minutes. He says that if I sees him around-like with a boxer of note and I am too shy to ask the said boxer for his autograph Mr Broadribb will get it for me. This is the first time anyone has ever offered to help me with my hobby. I also met Seaman Nobby Hall, the lightweight champion boxer of Europe. I was ever so clumsy. My boot grazed the highly polished surface of his left shoe. He was naturally angry and very nearly gave me his Hall mark – a knockout.

I am still working in the carpentry shop opposite The Camberwell Palace at Camberwell Green. I hate it. What is prospect, what is the future in being a slave to a horrible plaining machine ?

1922

This is a strange day. . . for my mother treated me – paid for me to go to the pictures with her. First time ever thats happened.

Yes, my mother paid. We saw a picture called *The Sheik*. The featured player is a bloke named Rudolph Valentino. I saw this man in a piece called *The Four Horsemen of the Apocalypse*, where he danced a very neat tango. Now he is all passionate, and girls go time after time to watch this bloke make love. My mother says he has IT. What IT is I dont know. But he makes love to Agnes Ayre in a very nice way. But I think anyone could make love to her. I would do that quite free, whereas Mr V. gets a lot of money for doing same.

If Mr Valentino had been in the flicker's place that afternoon I am very sure he would have got mobbed. What has he got ? White teeth. A very excellent well-shaped nose. Dark eyes. And he has a way with him. His real name is Rodolph Gugueleimi, and he is Italian. I am told that in private life he is a very unfriendly man with lots of self importance. Good luck to him. He *is* important. He interests ladies, and that is something I cannot do. E. M. Hull, who wrote the book from which this film was made, is no doubt very much obliged to R. V. for making this film. I am glad he made it, for otherwise I am very sure my mother would not have taken me. Lots of people seem to dislike Valentino, and I think that its only ENVY.

I am so very glad to tell you, diary, that I have got away from carpentry. Again a docter said it was killing me. At last I am my own master and I sell books – mostly from a sack. My mother says I am very stupid not to have a regular job, but as long as I pay her one pound a week for my keep I can go my own way. I am very very happy.

1923

I suppose that I really ought to put on record how I started the wonderfull game of bookselling. I went to a jumble sale at Denmark Hill, Camberwell and for eight shillings I bought all the books they had. I spent all the next day (a Sunday) cleaning them up and on Monday morning I took them out in a nice clean sack, over to Charing Cross Road, and inside two hours I had sold out – *and made a profit*. I took twenty four wonderfull shillings. I have been doing very much the same for this year. Not always so lucky. Sometimes Ive had to borrow two or three bob from my dad in order to pay my mother one pound a week, but Ive never once owed my dad more than three days. I am very happy. I find Rider Haggard and Marie Corelli and Mrs H. Wood to be the best of my sellers. I buy from barrows and I sell to shops. Its called 'Bookrunning'. . . only I *dont* run.

March 1924

Slowly but surely I am getting around where I can buy books at very cheap prices. I make a lot of mistakes, but on the whole I do sell my stock. I have to walk miles to find books. I find that the better the borough the cleaner the books. If I go to a rummage sale in Tooting or Streatham I get clean books. If I go to Bethnal Green they are ever so grubby, but the price asked is much the same.

I buy books mostly Fridays and Saturdays. I clean them Sundays. I sell on Mondays and Tuesdays. What do I do Wednesdays and Thursdays ? Well I mostly go on Wednesdays to public Libraries to learn about books and their values and on Thursdays I have a day off and I go out autograph collecting. I have now spoken to Arnold Bennett four times and got his signature twice. His is a very worth while autograph to get but he is not always in the mood to oblige. He can be very touchy. He suffers with bad head aches. I know that he likes to hear saucy jokes and the twice I got his autograph I was able to tell him pretty good funny tales. He didnt laugh – I aint never seen him really LAUGH – but he did grin.

This night as he waited for his car (it was a first night) he was for him a bit in a talkative mood and he told me a good tale. I best put this tale down before I go to sleep else I am sure to forget it. Arnold Bennett said, there was in a certain West End Club a cloak room attendent who possessed a very good memory and knew all the members of the club by sight. On one occasion a certain very noble gentleman handed over his overcoat to the attendant and was rather surprised that he didn't get a ticket for his coat, but said nothing. Later that evening the said noble bloke on leaving the club went back again to the attendant and was immediately handed over his correct overcoat. The noble gent then said to the attendent

'How did you know it was *my* coat ?'

'But I dont know if its *your* coat sir,' replied the attendent.

'Then why on earth did you give it to me ?' asked the noble man.

'Because thats the coat you gave to me to mind !'

Mr Bennett has a stammer. It spoils story telling – but he obviously told this one many times and it came out in his curious sweaky way almost pat. Its a jolly good tale. So far Ive never yet been anywhere where I've yet had to get anyone to mind my coat because most places I *sit* on it to make me *taller*.

I suppose I ought to put here that in lots of ways Arnold Bennett is odd. He has a curious way of walking and one shoulder seems higher than the other. His hair looks odd. His face looks odd and he has an uncommonly shaped nose and teeth like a *horse* ! He is a very great man for all his moods (he has headaches that are most *cruel* to him). As long as I dont make myself a worry and perhaps speak 3 times a year to him real *politely* I think I can keep in his good books. I can't do anything for him (except make him smile) but he can do a jolly lot for ME. *Old Wives Tales* and *The Card* are his best novels and some stories of his read good. The most powerfull living author – thats Mr Bennett, and he came up the hard way. Staffordshire must be proud of him. I'm real sorry he aint a fitter man. He is friends with E. M. Forster (I want this man's autograph !) and also of Eden Phillpotts (I've got his Autograph). Tonights meeting was at Court Theatre and *The Farmers Wife* by E. Phillpotts was on. It could have been off for all I cared : I couldn't understand all of the lingo. But lots of people laughed so I suppose half the audience know rustic language. I didnt laugh but I was satisfied for those 4 or 5 minutes with A.B. (as he waited for his car) made the journey worth while.

This is the first time I've been to the Court Theatre as its quite out of the way and when you get there, well, there is NO where else to go. I much prefer around Cambridge Circus 'cause then if you dont get autographs at one place in 15 minutes you can rush off to another theatre and perhaps be more lucky. . . but where can you rush to after The Court ? Nowhere ! Near Victoria Station a well built lady asked if I had change for 6d. I had. I gave her 12 halfpennies. She said it was 'No good.' No Good for *what* ? I asked her – and she didn't reply.

I am still bookselling – mostly by a sack of stock. I'm making a living. My mothers ceased to complain. My dad is pleased with me. I am pleased with myself. I am still HAPPY.

June 1925

Arnold Bennett said this evening in my hearing (although *not* to me) that 2 young men of today would matter a great deal TOMORROW. They were Aldous Huxley and Noël Coward. It was pretty obvious that he had a considerable amount of admiration for both of them. The lady to whom he said this then asked when was tomorrow – and Bennett said nothing. I felt he wanted to say *something* – something bright and witty but could not get his tongue round the words his mind had given birth too. It occurred to me that both Coward and Huxley would have made a quick reply to this woman. Of course, we *all* know that tomorrow never comes but we all know what Bennett *means*. I dont have much admiration for Aldous Huxley because in truth 3 parts of what he writes is quite over my head and I cannot make head nor tale of it. Yes, its FINE literature but too fine for me. However, it sells and thats all that *really* matters. On the other hand I really enjoyed *Fallen Angels* and its real good Theatre by any standard. I have not met Noël Coward to speak to yet – but it is a treat for the future. I often see him around and he seems really amiable. I dont expect any trouble when I ask him for *his* autograph as being in the theatre all his life he must realise that it is a very cheap but admirable form of publicity – and whereas the abrupt refusal of an autograph can make an admirer into a hater, the granting can click the admiration and make it last.

I've now spoken 6 times to A. Bennett and got amiability each time. He looks downright poorly, like as if he works far too hard and yet he must be a very very rich man. Surely he can afford 6 months entire rest. Seems the richer and more important you are in the world of letters the *harder you work* ! Probably its contracts. Maybe it advances on books yet to be written. But it seems downright bloody silly. I dont suppose Noël Coward writes himself to a standstill or when he's poorly *still* works. I am sure Mr Huxley looks after himself as well. But Bennett who could be their father and you'd think the *wisest* man in London is *not wise at all* and is working himself into hospital – if not worse. Its strange ! As for me, diary, I am doing ever so nicely, Thank you.

August 1925

Valentino is dead. There is only one Valentino. I reckon there will only always be *one* Valentino. . . I have never since I first saw him in pictures 5 years ago (*4 Horsemen*) found much to rave over and I much prefer Tom Mix, W. S. Hart and William Farnum – but then I aint a woman. Pola Negri will be knocked out by his death – and so will Alice and Mary in this street. They are both 15 and I know they've sat *all* day 2 days in a week seeing a Valentino picture – took their food with them and a bottle of milk. I'd like Mary for me 'dinah' but she wont look at me. Valentino wont make no more pictures so perhaps I'll get chance ! Perhaps lots of men will get their wives back into their loving arms now the Prince of Lovers dead ! But Cinema owners and makers must be bit sad this day. They have lost a gold mine.

I am finding a small gold mine. I buy novels size 7½x5 (called crown 8vo) and I sell them mostly to public Libraries, its a living. I make 35/- clear profit a week with luck. Must have luck.

I am happy selling books, suits me proper nicely.

Sunday, 7th February 1926

This afternoon I went to a charity concert organised by Sybil Thorndyke and my seat cost 1s. 2d. in the gallery at The Alhambra in Charing X Road. It helped The Childrens Country Holiday Fund. I went to this concert because the first time I ever had a holiday or saw the sea was at the age of 10 under the auspices of this here said fund so I *know* they do good work.

It was a full house and only gallery seats were to be had. The stars in the concert included May Huxley, a nice singer (I heard all her words right up in 'the Gods'). Then Ernest Butcher and Muriel George gave us more songs. They were followed by Layton and Johnstone 2 coloured singers – who got the best applause of the day and were a really perfect team. Eva Moore then gave a couple of recitations but, alas, I could not hear much what she was reciting. Talbot O'Farrell then really entertained us with some quite funny stories – mostly Irish. He is a big man of some 6 ft 2 and 16 stone and a voice to match this weight. He could be heard all over the building – indeed, probably in the street as well ! The afternoon finished with Jack Hylton and his Band playing in brilliant style. No doubt this is Britain's favourite Band – for one very good reason : they play what you *hope* they'll play ! The programme cost 1s. (also for the Funds) and my copy was sold to me by Vera Pearce, a big lady on the stage. I've seen her twice front ways but never had time to walk round her ! I got her to autograph my programme. When the show was over I waited and Sybil Thorndyke obliged me with also signing the same programme. She had on a most outrageous looking hat and didnt look a bit stylish – but when you are such a star I suppose it dont matter so much about dress ! Anyrate, she was a proper real lady and *thanked me* for asking her !

14th February 1926

Today I went to The Palladium at Oxford Circus and I heard The Royal Albert Hall orchestra conducted by Sir Landon Ronald. It could, of course, have been The Pallidium Orchestra at the Albert Hall but it wasnt. I feel more at ease and so enjoy good music *more* at The Pallidum. Todays programme consisted of

CARNEVAL by Dvorak
Passepied from Le Roi S'amuse. Delibes
Pianoforte Concerto in B Flat. Tchaikovsky
Unfinished Symphony. Schubert (Why dont some one finish this bit ?)
Suite Peer Gynt. Grieg

I call this a lovely balanced prog and it cost only 2s. for a very good seat. I didn't pay this sum. A poet friend thought I ought to hear Peer Gynt – at least Sir Landon Ronald's interpretation of it – so he took me. The solo pianist at this concert was a gentleman named *Sapellnikoff*. I'm sure he was a gentleman to *stand* such a jaw cracking name. I did not attempt to get his autograph in case he asked me to pronounce it. But I did capture Sir Landon Ronald and he turned out to be a really nice amiable man. He was interested to know that I'd turned up for Peer Gynt and said that it was 'music of a life time' (which I think is a nice phrase). He also said Tchaikovsky was a very strange man – amongst the strangest and greatest composers the world will ever know. Sir Landon wrote a few notes of music above his autograph. And *didnt* see the joke when I said 'By these notes I will remember you.' He didn't smile. I did not see Sapellnikoff. He had knicked off. I enjoyed myself today – I always do when I listen to really good music.

7th March 1926

The Shakespeare Memorial Theatre at Stratford on Avon was today destroyed by fire. This is sad news. The Library and picture gallery were saved after a long fight and the folios and quartos were removed in time. The roof of the Theatre caved in after the fire had been going 2 hrs and then the tower went. Its all a hopeless mess now so I am told and although I've never been there or seen anything of the Theatre Johnston Forbes Robertson told me much about it. I expect it will soon be rebuilt – but its sad. 'There are some things insurance money can never replace and that's *atmosphere*.' These are F-R's words.

13th May 1927

Today Mr Noël Coward has sent me a signed photograph. I suppose he is the most talked about man in the theatre world today. I do think he is brilliant. I can do all that he can do only not so good – and I do not expect I shall ever be *quite* so good. The girls rave about him. He isn't handsome. He isn't snobbish. He is amiable, not a bit 'starchy'. I will tell you, diary, that I *do* admire him. If I wasn't me, I rather think that I'd like to be him with a world of lovely ladies at his feet and he can have his choice. Do I envy him ? Yes, I bloody well do ! . . . But I am happy. I hope Mr Coward is as happy this lovely day.

19th August 1927

I am off to Hamburg tomorrow for a gamble in cigarette cards. I feel that some one must bring back some of the glorious series of cards now in German packets. I will also see German women who have a lot of IT, all in the right places. Frank says that German women are tough and cold and rather ruthless, and the only way to capture them is by sheer brutality. They adore only the CAVE MEN. . . I will gamble 10 pounds on cigarette cards and two pounds on a cold lump of German femininity – which I hope to warm up. Well, its all experience ! This is only a 4 day jaunt, just to Hamburg. I will leave Berlin for another year or two.

5 hours later. I have on sound advice changed my mind and instead of Hamburg I am going 4 days to Ostend. I am told it is possible to get cards there – not actually in cigarette packets but from a card manufacturer and printers. This suits me better than to buy unrequired cigarettes in order to get required samples of European cards. I am also informed that the females of Ostend are a great deal warmer and very much *cheaper*.

24th August 1927

The jaunt to Ostend did not prove to be a success in any way. The printing firm would not at any price (and I mean any price) supply me with sample sets of cards. I was very disappointed. I was disappointed in the women as well. They were ever so mercenary. I have never come upon women so mercenary. Its almost as if they have a complete scale of charges. 2s. for a kiss. 2s. 6d. if they kissed you. 5s. for one hand on bust, and so on. All night was average price of two English pounds (although one girl wanted £3 – but she was very handsome with merry eyes). I did *not* have even two shillings worth. Oh yes, they all seemed warm but I refused to pay 40s. to stoke up the fire ! Instead, I had several card games behind the Casino (not *in* the Casino). I WON money, but they would not allow me to take out what I had won in cash, only in kind. So I had a box of cigars. There were 50 in the box and they cost roughly 6d. each. They said if I broke the seal and used a couple they'd be no customs trouble (and they were right). I also got a small bottle of 3 star Martell back. The whole trip cost roughly £12. I learnt one thing. Ask the scale of charges and the timing of the scales *before* ever getting acquainted with Flemish Women! We live to learn.

August 1927

Its a very funny thing when one comes to think of it (if anyone but me would) that the largest sized photograph I've yet had from a star has come from Wee Georgie Wood, the smallest size star I've come upon. He also had what looked the Biggest size in cars and a very large lady as company. Of course, being small made the car and the lady larger, but truly they were large. And now – now he's sent me a large size cabinate photo. Is it something what is called phyciological what causes these things to happen? A very large wrestler wrote his name in tiny letters. A very buxom variety star sent a photo the exact size of an ordinary cigarette card. Mr Wood is an extremely nice amiable man (he isn't what one would call a boy in age although he certainly is in looks). I like him better than Ivor Vintor who is also a little man and here is why. Georgie looks, acts, speaks and lives as a *boy* – whilest Mr Vintor is just a miniature *man*. There *is* a difference.

October 1927

A funny old bloke gave me a photo tonight. He is Sam Mayo. He is on The Halls. It was all very strange. I was trying to get quite another man. I made a mistake. I asked this man Sam Mayo and he seemed very surprised. When he'd signed he got a photo from his inside pocket and that was already signed and gave it to me as well. He said he was very pleased to have been asked for his autograph. He had carried a photo about in his pocket for many years hoping someone would ask him ! He said he thought he was a back number – and now I had asked. He gave me 7s. all in one shillings. I did *not* want to take it. He was not drunk either ! He has a very ordinary face and, like me, he wears a cap. On The Halls he looks miserable. But he was real friendly. I am glad I asked this man Sam Mayo. My mother says he is a foundation stone of real British music hall. That is praise. He said he'd promised to give all the money in his right hand pocket to the first to ask for his autograph. And that was *me* !

1927

A man named Lindbergh has flown the Atlantic and there is lots of mad excitement. Me, I *can't* see it as wonderful (and me, I don't envy the man at all.) All I says is if you have a reliable plane, enough petrol, ability to get that plane up and ability to get it down again, *all* you have to do is get up, sit up, don't fall asleep and when you got no more petrol come down and that way you can fly two Atlantics ! Its just a matter of keeping awake. And now I'll go to *sleep* and dream about Gloria Swanson.

30th August 1928

Needing a little material for an article I was writing on the stage for a club magazine, I wrote to Jean Forbes Robertson asking her two very civil questions. She has now kindly replied. . . and how ! (This is an American expression Ive just heard and it seems to fit.) What is your hobby? Answer : PIANO. Just that one word. Does she mean sell them, make them, polish 'em or play them ? Maybe she likes to listen to 'em. How am *I* to know ?

And the second question. If you was not on the stage what would you like to be ? Answer : A SAILOR. Well, I suppose if you asks silly questions you are entitled to get silly blooming answers.

I wont ask her again, I might get a one word answer.

But she is a nice actress . . . sometimes.

27th September 1928

Tonight I went to the Piccadilly Theatre (just off Piccadilly Circus) and I saw *The Jazz Singer* which is a talking film. As you *see* the man singing you *hear* the man singing. If it wasn't that the noise sort of blares forth like 20 gramophones at once or six strong voices singing at once it would be a *miracle*. I suppose really it *is* a miracle. I had front row and I got a bad headache through looking up at the screen. If this had been a real live show my seat would have been 'best in the house'. As it was talking cinema it was *worst* in the *cinema*. Still, I ought not to say nothing, because Edgar Wallace (of all people) gave me this ticket. He just said 'Perhaps you can use this ?' Ever so calm he said it. When I saw what this was I was flabagasted with joy. All the stars was there. I got eleven autographs – plus an ache in my neck and a real sickening headache. A. Jolson is the Jazz Singer. I dont like him : Sings Awfull.

6th January 1929

I've had such a strange letter from Leonard Merrick in Wiesbaden. Here it is (forgive me, Mr Merrick, I *have* to repeat it) :

> Dear Freddie Bason,
>
> I am sorry I cannot give you my autograph because I am very busy at the moment but here is my signature.
>
> Yours very truly,
>
> Leonard Merrick

And it isn't even April the First. Strange thing is that I *never* asked for his autograph ! His books are all edited and introduced by famous authors. I will have my books introduced in the same way some day. That way you get *two* lots of readers, the introducer's and your own !

1929

I have seen John Geilgud as Hamlet. I had been told that it was a 'must' for the sake of my education. Charles Morgan says it is a tour de force. At least it sounded just like that. Mr Morgan is an extremely educated man, I am not. Was it great acting ? Oh yes it was undoubtedly great acting, but I've just got to be absolutely honest, diary, I was *not* moved by Mr Geilgud's Hamlet. I was very young when I was taken to see John Barrymore in Hamlet and then I was moved. Halfway through Mr Geilgud's Hamlet, I had severe stomach pains – and went home *un*moved.

November 1930

Maugham has just gone home after a visit here. I wasn't able to put down anything of our conversation because it wasn't an interview but a friendly visit. I cannot help feeling that I ought to put down some things he said. Maybe no one will ever read them but what does that matter ? In my old age, I shall read them and they will bring back memories to me. As near as is humanly possible, here are just three things he said.

1. Very few people are suitable to put into fiction. My characters are at times suggested by people I know, but I've never modelled them on living people. By the time the book is completed, there is very little left of the original and I mean practically *nothing* left of the original.

2. He also said that no one was so rounded as to be suitable for fiction. I asked what he meant by rounded – and he said, 'They have odd corners that would stick out in a book.'

3. One of my favorite characters of those I've invented is Thorp Athelny. You will find him in *Of Human*

Bondage. He's gay and rather unscrupulous. Yes, I like him.

Ain't much after an hour with Somerset Maugham, but then a little is lots better than nothing. He brought a lovely pair of boots for me or my father. I feel like putting 'em in a glass case. They are his cast-offs ! Too big for me. Will my dad (who aint *ever* read a book in all his life) appreciate standing in Willie's shoes? For myself, I want to stand on my own two feet – not be propped up by anyone – ever. All I want to do is become a modern Samuel Pepys. He is very famous and very dead. I am not a ¼ dead yet.

November 1930

Tonight I went to The Hackney Empire, one of the best of variety houses, to see a pal of mine (Kimberley) and was graciously allowed to stand awhile in the wings and look at the acts. One of them was a magician. He asked for any lady in the audience to go up on the stage and he would make her disappear. A chap in the audience shouted out 'Wait 5 minutes and I will go and get my old woman.' The magician ignored this and continued. 'I will bring the disappearing lady back *unharmed*.' And the man in the audience said 'Bring her back ! No fear ! *Anyone* can do *that* !'

I hope this man was not a planted man (called a stooge) – but that this was a genuine sample of Hackney humour. I remember a time – oh, all of ten years ago – two boxers were taking it easy in round 6 of a 8 rd. contest and some one in the gallery called out 'For Gord's sake *kiss* him ! Make him mad ! Tickle him !' The boxers almost together looked in the direction this voice had come from – but the boxer from Clapham had quicker reflexes and turned his eyes back quickly and saw his opponent was *not looking at him* so up went a solid right hook – bang on the jaw.

His opponent was absolutely knocked out cold. I often wondered if that was a put up job ! After all, it *would* be a way to win a crooked fight. I do hope the man at the Hackney Empire wasn't in the magician's employment – and I *dont* want to find out !

17th March 1930

I have nearly completed my book about Gallerites and The Gods which is to be called *Gallery Unreserved* and will be published next year with an introduction by Mr W. S. Maugham. Although I have myself a mine of quite good stage stories for it that I've so far not tapped I had a feeling that I ought to try to get some other folks to contribute a story or two. Now, having some admiration of Eden Phillpotts (who's two plays *Farmer's Wife* and *Yellow Sands* made him a fortune and contributed to the mirth of the nation) I felt he would be a sure one to know a good stage tale, so I wrote him a nice letter asking if he could recall a theatre tale from his vast (40 years) experience of the stage. I also sent him a mint copy of a first edition of *Children of the Mist* which I was sure would delight him. I felt I could not pay him in *cash* but his own book would be in kind. Today I got a postcard from him. It just says : 'I have nothing interesting and amusing to tell you on the subject of the theatre, otherwise I would gladly do so. E.P.' Just signed E.P. but the whole written by him. Well, that's amusing and interesting, isn't it – I mean the card in itself (although he could have said 'Thank you' for the bleedin BOOK). Bless his heart, he must be shy. I mean to say, I ain't half his age yet I've heard over 150 really funny stage tales. Well, I have his initials although not his autograph. But surely it only takes 2 seconds to add -den to E, hillpotts to the P. I will not ask anyone else for stories. When your cert favourite loses by a length its best to give up ! But, oh, how I enjoyed *Yellow Sands*. I paid seven times to see it and I'm *still* a E— P— admirer. I suppose the moral is *dont* ask a fellow author to help fill your book ! And *dont* help fill anyone elses book either. Refuse all such requests. But NO, I *wont* do that (signed) F— B—.

Winter 1931

My Diary, there comes a time in every man's life when suddenly he realises that he is *no* longer unknown – that try as he may, he can no longer bury his head in the sand and think of himself as an unknown nobody. This point in my life came yesterday. There came to my door a reporter from a well known newspaper together with a camera man. The reporter asked for a ten minutes or so interview and permission to take my photograph.

Now I know its ever so good for one's ego to be interviewed and photographed but it is publicity which often leaves an entirely *false* impression with the rest of the world. They have a foolish idea that because you are famous, you are rich and because you are well known you are nearly rich. I wanted no false impression to get around that I was getting famous even in a small way so I said to the reporter almost as a joke, 'For how much, sir ?' He asks what did I mean. I explained that it was really quite simple. I am not Ivor Novello or Godfrey Tearle. I am just a product of the slum named Fred Bason, and I wanted to know how much I was to be paid *in cash* to go to my bedroom, put on my best suit, have a hurried shave, put hair cream on my hair and return here inside 10 minutes with a bright smile on my face !

'But we don't need any preparation like *that*. We want you *as you are* !'

'As I am, untidy and *not* partically fresh ! I *refuse* to be presented to an unknown public looking like a tramp. This is the first time a newspaper has ever wanted me photo or my views and if I am going to make a start it will be a start on the way I mean to go on. I dont like snapshots. If you cant take a nice Sunday photo on a Friday, then I will give you one already done !'

That didn't suit them. They would *wait*. They waited 22 minutes for me. When I returned I did look reasonably presentable so the interview began. I did not say anything at all shattering. I think they expected much more and me to be *ever* so 'Gor Blimey'. But 2 days later I got the 21s. Why did I *charge* ? Ivor Novello advised it ! When I get advice from men who know their onions I use it and *act on it*.

A black tie for Arnold Bennett, 1931

I think that in 8 or 9 years I've spoken perhaps 20 times to Arnold Bennett. It would be impudent if I put here, diary, that we were friends. He was amiable to me at all times. He was downright kind. Perhaps it would be fair to say only that he befriended me as a mountain shades a tiny bush from the sun. We only went out once together when I took him over to Lambeth to 'The Beggar's Theatre' (where Buskers try out their acts on fellow Buskers).

But now he is dead and I feel very very unhappy. He's been looking ill for years and I can't recall *ever* seeing him look fit. He suffered with headaches and lack of sleep. He overworked for years and years.

He knew where I lived. He told me he had seen my house on his way through to Bromley one afternoon. Bennett was a real good kind man – one of the best loved literary figures in the *whole* world (and I mean the whole world). They put straw down in the road to deaden the sound of the traffic as he lay dying. They dont do that in Baker Street unless you are very very great !

But what always astonished me was that Mr Bennett had a bauldy mind. Tell him a downright dirty tale and he could cap it. Ive met a lot of writers in the past 7 or 8 years, but none for whom I had more respect than Enoch

Arnold Bennett. He was never pompous or fussy. He would listen. He was interested.

He knew the value of his autograph in a book. He knew I'd sell it eventually, but so long as I told him a real good joke he would sign and the better the joke, the bigger the inscription. It was good whilst it lasted – and now it is no more. *Old Wives Tales,* signed by him, paid for a month at Brighton for my mother after she had a heart attack. I never told him this. *Journalism for Women* and *Lord Raingo* signed by him gave my father £8 – which he lost betting on horses (still, it kept him happy). 3 copies of *Accident* signed by Bennett paid for 2 weeks at Southend for me. He would have agreed I put it all to good use. Now all I have is a final copy of *Accident* and 9 letters from Bennett to me. These I will *never* sell. I will wear a black tie for a month in memory of A.B.

March 1932

The boxing at the Royal Albert Hall was marred with a great tragedy tonight, because during the fight between Larry Gains and Don McCorkindale for the British Empire Heavyweight title Jack Goodwin (probably the greatest trainer in the history of British boxing) died whilst in Larry Gains' corner. I possess Jack Goodwin's book *Myself and My Boxers* and have often been on the point of getting Mr Goodwin to autograph it for me. But seeing him around all the time, I just didn't bother for it never seemed urgent and it wasn't as if he was only seldom in London. He was a pillar of London boxing with a finger in most of the pies. And now he is dead. God rest his soul. I did not know him personally at all. He did once allow me into a gym to see a work-out when someone else was going to bar me admission which was kind of him. He died in harness which I suppose was what he would have wished, if anyone had troubled to ask him. His death tonight has taught me one thing : *Never* put off for tomorrow the autographs I can get today – because tomorrow may not come – either for the celebrity *or for me* !

October 1932

It was my delight today to have luncheon with John Drinkwater, the notable Author. He is a tall and striking looking man. He is the first man I've seen since R Brook who *looks* like a poet. He does write poems but I have not read any of them. I never seem to enjoy any poetry except that of W. B. Yeats. John was kind enough to sign five of his books for me. Having just signed his name to them I then pointed out that they were worth 2s. 6d. *un*signed. 6s. just signed. 7s. 6d. 'With Best wishes' *and* signed, 12s. 6d. a copy with a 3 lines inscription and if he made them 4 and 6 lines presentation inscription I could very probably get 15s. a copy for them ! He was astounded at this information and said that it was an EYE opener and as I taught him something (he didnt say what) he would try to give me a *13s. 6d.* inscription in each volume and then, bai jove, he took 20 minutes to write ever such long inscriptions. 2 were 6 lines each and 3 had 3 long lines of at least 26 words collectively. He is a darling man. I could never picture Walpole doing this ! Mr Drinkwater doesnt like Mr Walpole and neither do I.

John showed me his stamp collection and its a pretty noble one. I would say 1,500 pounds wouldn't pay for it. He belongs to several stamp clubs and knows a great deal about stamps. Advises me to Buy Penny Black at 5s. each and by 1962 they will be 25s. each. But I'd rather bet 5s. on a greyhound and win or lose at *once* than wait 30 years for a quid. All in all a really enjoyable afternoon. 3 cheers for an amiable Author.

1932

In the Foyer of the Ivy Restaurant John Galsworthy tonight spared a few minutes to chat to me. One thing about

Galsworthy is sure, he is very much a gentleman. He is everything that I would expect in a gentleman and we who write should be so proud of Galsworthy (I expect we are).

He told me a tale which is well worth recording here. There was a chap who was writing his first novel. He had worked a long time on it and was half way through his masterpiece when one afternoon he found his boy age 6 was most carefully putting it page by page on the fire! He was most angry and was just going to thrash his son when a friend called. When told about the burnt novel the friend said 'Can your son read?'

'Oh yes, he reads very well for his age.'

It turned out that his son had read the unfinished manuscript and hadn't liked it at all – so he'd BURNT it! Mr Galsworthy assured me that it actually happened.

Mr Galsworthy said that the older he got the more illegible became his writing. But he's prepared to write every word, rather than dictate. He said he would never been a Dictator. He autographed one of his works for me – in his usual kind manner – and gave me permission to sell it 'at best possible price' when the need arises. It keeps on arising! Its quite a struggle to make a living and yet still people will pay fantastic prices for the scarcer first editions. I shall never really know why a first edition of *Men of Property* is worth around 80 pounds when the 2nd impression of this same novel isn't worth 8s. I dont even think supply and demand has really much to do with it! It is a fad and we who sell must cater for this fad. I shall get four times more for Mr G's novel solely because he's autographed it—yet if he put his name on a postcard and I stuck the postcard in the Book I would be lucky to get 2s. 6d. more. Yes, his autograph is worth 2s. 6d. in the autographic market right now as against 7s. 6d. for Maugham and 25s. for G. B. Shaw. On the other hand Noël Coward's signature is worth 1s. in cash but more usefull as a swop. The signature of R. M. Ayres, a writer of love tales, is also worth 1s. Its a strange world. If it was Mr A. Lincoln's signature then it becomes worth upwards of 25 *pounds* !

April 1933

Without comment ! A friend in New York sent me a card to say that a lovely blonde and a handsome young man held a KISS for 3 hours and 2 minutes at Coney Island, N.Y. this week and won a loving cup for the worlds endurance title for Kissing !

I say 'without comment' – but really I suppose I ought to add of *course* it was in U.S.A. Nowhere else would any man waste so much time on *one* kiss with *one* blonde.

November 1933

This evening at The Garrick Theatre (of all places) learning that Jimmy Wilde, one time celebrated Boxer, would be there I took up to the Theatre 5 fighting photos of the said Gallant Jimmy taken at the height of his fame and asked him for 'Old times sake' to oblige by autographing them. Then to my dismay I found I'd lost my pen and he hadn't one either. He took the photos however and stamped addressed envelope and assured me he would post them back to me in a day or so. He is now a tubby man and must be all of 9 st. 6 pound. His real fighting weight was 7 st. 6. (He was always far inside the flyweight limit.) His power was in his fist : he punched *double* his weight. Joe Conn told me that once when fighting Wilde he got a punch that seemed to go *through* him. Conn was absolutely paralized by the pain and the power of it and thought it was a sledge hammer instead of a spider arm that threw such a stunning punch. Joe Conn said that in all his career (many hundreds of fights) he had never had such a punch – he felt its effect weeks later.

1933

I've found a kind, friendly, modest, gentle author. It's so strange to find such a great number of virtues in *one* man. His name is Roland Pertwee who wrote *Interference* – and he writes topping tales as well. If I ever become famous please God, I carry my bit of fame as gently as Mr Pertwee.

September 1933

This is ever so odd. Yesterday a woman in Chelsea died after drinking about 3 ozs of Eucalyptus neat. What puzzels me is why why the hell she wanted to drink the bleeding stuff. Didnt she have a chest to *rub* it on ? They do daft things in Chelsea but this is the sillest. Said to be the first known case of death by Eucalyptus. Maybe in this fact there may be the theme for a clever murder mystery *The Eucalyptus Death*. But I must not make jest of this sad tragedy. I expect she mistook the bottle for cough mixture !

12th November 1933

For a treat I shut up shop of selling Books today and went to Sothebys and saw a good Book sold. It was a Shakespeare folio owned by Major G. H. Vernon and although it had several minor defects it realised 2,800 pounds. This copy had been in the Vernon family since almost the day it was published which makes this family a pretty old one. American collectors have recently carried off to U S A all the folios. Only recently Gabriel Wells paid 14,500 pounds for a particully fine first folio. But looking round Sothebys today I didnt see a man who looked American in any way and I believe this copy *will* stay in England. Perhaps the Americans had been warned that the Vernons *read* their Shakespeare thousands of times since it had been in its family hence its defects ! Maybe the Americans only want it mint in dust wrapper ? Or perhaps they prefer it autographed by Bacon ? Still £2,800 for a very worn shabby copy is a jolly good price – keep me in Bacon the rest of my life !

3rd January 1934

I am in a bit of a quandary (probably spelt that word wrong). I'm in a Hell of a fix. I want to oblige Arthur Rackham, the great artist. Anyone would want to oblige Rackham, there aint a kinder, more amiable artist in all the world. He's living at Stilegate, near Limpsfield, in Surrey and he is coming up to London to see me soon. He wants to buy books on old pottery and old glass with *plenty* of illustrations in them ! I haven't had a Book on *either* in ten years ! Now this is the fix : if I go over to Putney or Chiswick or into the West End of London to shops where they have good stocks of the books Rackham needs, I will have to pay anything from 30s. to 3 guineas per copy. Well, say I speculate 35s. on a Book on Old Glass. Supposing he has it already, or it doesn't *quite* fulfill his requirements, or the price isn't *just* right, or ten or twelve other 'ifs' and 'buts', and he turns it down, I am left with this book on my hands and I have never ever before had a request for a book on pottery or glass (or even porcelain for that matter). I don't know a soul in this world who will buy it from me if Mr Rackham doesn't !

Some people think they have but to ask and low and behold a bookseller gets their requirements. You *cannot* pick up books on pottery at 6d. each ! Such a book can change hands six or seven times before it reaches its buyer and each time at a slightly higher price – each one getting a 'nibble at the bun'. You can search a dozen shops and fail to find an authorative book on pottery. Booksellers are not mugs. I am not a know-all, but I'd know that a good book on rare glass would make slightly higher than 1s. 6d. ! As I've been writing this bit today, I've come to the conclusion that there is only *one* way to oblige Mr Rackham and that's to tell him where he can go and see and select for *himself*. I will give him three addresses where he can see over two hundred and under two hundred and fifty books collectively, in those shops, that are 'up his street'. And why shall I do this? I'll tell you. He drew a painting for me – a darling little chicken as a Christmas card – all for me – unasked. He could have got £5 for it from almost anyone who collects his work. I cannot let him down – but it *is* a quandary – or a heck of a fix – isn't it?

10th January 1934

A lady who is Jimmy Wilde's sister in Law has sent back my 5 fighting pictures. She found them in one of her trunks when she returned home from a holiday with the Wildes. Fortunately they were all signed. Aint it funny how things turn up in such strange places? And I'd written Jimmy twice for them and he wondered where he'd put them. Alls well that ends well.

10th January 1935

This day I purchased *Ego* by James Agate for myself. I dont care if I sell it or not. I hope some day that I can compile my own *Ego* but not so much about things as people. People will always be interested in people but things are quite another Kettle of Fish. A lot about Golf when I have no interest whatsoever in Golf would put me off a book. Ive known people who before they purchased a book of recollections looked down the index and if they didnt know very well at least 30% of the folks put the book down again. The only books of recollection that I rather dislike are those of titled ladies who in their 70's and 80's remember back 60 and 70 years ago and seem to absolutely scrape the Barrell of memory just in order to bring in a name which was well known in their childhood and so put that name in the index. For instance I came upon a book which said – 'and I *thought* I saw Lord Tennyson there.' And, blow me down, Tennyson was in the index as large as life ! Being famous doesnt necessarily mean that a man is *interesting*. Many really famous names in the peerage are very dull old men. . . .

If I had my way and if I had the money to back my judgement I would be a publisher of just ONE sort of Book (apart from my own). I would get every really great film star under contract to me to write one book. Just think of the very interesting things that folks like William S. Hart, Mary Pickford, D. Fairbanks, Charlie Chaplin, Francis Ford, Eddie Polo and a host of others could write or could have written. Film history in the making. . . So often boxers and cricketters remember – but what a lot Mary Pickford can remember and I am sure it would be enchanting reading. But, of course, there has to be the *will* to write and the *ability* to put it all down ! I've got the will and Ive been putting it all down since I was 14. James Agate has both the ability and the will and I'm going to have a happy week this week reading his *Ego* but I wish it had been by Ronald Coleman instead !

July 1935

I've been today to Lords and watched a cricket match. It was a very boring affair. All I had to do was watch *cricket* and I *did* get bored. Oh I know this is the same thing said twice – but never mind. No one should ever mind my grammar. I must put down an observation. Does a man *have* to have an old school tie in order to be a 1st grade cricketter ? I will never go back to Lords. Its quite out of my line of sport. I can watch boxing and not for a moment be fed up but cricket – oh dear NO. I heard one thing there. Yes at Lords. 'Death is only going from one room into another. The door opens and you enter. The passing from one room to another is often *quite pleasant*.'

This said during an important cricket match. You couldnt ever ever think of such a thing being said whilst, say, Jack Peterson was having a go at The Albert Hall !

9th January 1936

Ive had a perfectly enjoyable night tonight. I went to see Noël Coward's *Tonight at 8.30* but it was *past* 8.30 when it started. I think Mr Coward must be the most envied man in Britain's stageland and yet, dash it all, he's earnt his fame the hard way – by sheer inspiration and perspiration. . .

I got several Autographs tonight – but on getting home I find that they are duplicates. It would seem that Noël Coward shows draw almost the *same* stars to shine in the foyer on each occasion. Somehow I *don't* think they are Mr Coward's friends for one overhears such down right catty things said on these occasions.

I hear Mr R. Kipling is ill. I can feel no sorrow for him. He was a really unkind man to me. I was so utterly polite when I asked for his signature and there was *only* me – it wasn't as if there was a crowd. And he lifted his stick to hit me. I said 'Kipling or No Bloody Kipling, if you hit me with that stick I'll Kipple *you*.' And I *ment* it.

25th May 1936

Today at Sothebys they are selling a vast collection of letters etc. from and to Arnold Bennett. I will not go. I know if I do I shall buy items which I will just hoard and its not a bit of use hoarding. When one is a collector of my magpie nature its like parting with a tooth to part with a treasure. I find I have near a dozen letters from Bennett. Why add to them ?

I must record my deep respect and everlasting admiration of Arnold Bennett – a truly great man. When he had something cutting to say of a person book or play he got it over very quickly and didn't linger or jump with joy on the victim ! He had a kindly heart and an army of genuine friends. What more can one say ? It is indeed an etipaph in itself. . .

I will not go to Sothebys. I get too excited, and let my sentimentality rule my slim purse.

July 1937

I'm so glad I accepted advice and bought by Nils Holstius a book called *Hollywood Through The Back Door*. It is a real eye opener for any one who thinks the *back* door to cinema fame is easy. You have to have credits and fame to get in by the front door to Hollywood. Untill I read this book I had a feeling that the back door might be unguarded and in some extremely humble capacity one might get in and rise. But it would seem that the only rise you get that way is either to have the rise taken out of you by that glorious invention called 'The Runaround', where appointments are made and *never* kept, where promises are made and never *ment* to be keepted, or you get a rise from some ones boot !

Its a *great* book. I've never before heard of Nils Holstius. I wonder that with a maze of Hollywood information in his book he did not put how Hollywood got its name ! Ive never put it down and I feel this is the place to put it down – the facts as told to ME by J. Turner a resident of Hollywood.

Mrs Evans was visiting Kansas from England on an American tour. Mrs Evans meet Mrs Wilcox who lived in Cahuenga Valley. They became friendly and Mrs Evans told her American friend all about her English home which was called Holly Wood and had holly trees around it. Mrs Wilcox enjoyed the company of her English friend and wanting a name for her own rather large farm in Cahuenga Valley and liking the name Holly Wood had a sign painted with that name on it – as a remembrance of her chance meeting with Mrs Evans. Mr Wilcox had some holly trees sent to him but they failed to live – only the name board remained. More houses sprang up around the Wilcox farm and it became almost a village around 'Holly Wood' – so they called that particular section of the Valley – Holly Wood. Yes, so simple !

I've twice tried to check on Mr Turner's historical data and no one disputes it so probally *lots* of people know of it !

Mr Holstius got the run-around in Hollywood for six months – getting exactly no where ever so slowly. He had remarkable patience. I would not have stuck 6 weeks of appointments never keepted and promises of help that were just so much talk. The cinema world is indeed a very harsh and cruel world and always ALWAYS you have to show a brave face and say you are doing well – even if you have only 6d. and are starving ! But as it is in Hollywood so it is in Charing X Road ! If the theatrical people of London dont put up a brave front and a smile they are *done*. Fortunately in the world of letters its not so bad. You dont have to act a part and no one cares how you live – just so long as you eventually fulfill your contract and dont ask for too big an advance ! I am glad I am not an actor and Ive *no* wish for Cinema fame.

To be a second Mr Pepys will suit me proper lovely. But it *has* a snag. I see it. I will have to sell myself. No one will read my Diaries (if anyone will ever be *brave* enough to publish them) untill they know of *me*. Its me first. Well, one thing's blooming sure I wont mimic Shaw and his antics. He eats vegetables and dont like meat. I *do* like meat and I'm not a one for potatoes as they lay on my chest. . .

Which brings me right to me again. I *did* have indigestion today. An American visitor wanted a fish and chips meal 'for the fun of it'. I had to keep him company (and pay the bill). Well, we had fish and chips and the chips was awfull and gave me indigestion. The Things I do for

England. My visitor was quite unaffected and got a 'kick' out of fish and chips. I thought you only got a 'kick' out of OPIUM.

On cigarette cards. 1937

On and off for a great many years I've collected cigarette cards. At one time I made a good deal of money out of cards one way or another. I would say roughly speaking that there are about 5,000 genuine cartophilists in Gt Britain today. Cartophily is the hobby of collecting cards and those who collect them are cartophilists. Many many times on my way up to the West End to collect autographs I've hunted the streets for empty cigarette cartons in the hope of finding cards in them. I must record that to find 6 to 10 cards in one evening is quite a haul. Its an inexpensive hobby and the information on the back of the cards has given me a wider knowledge than I would have got had I not come into the card game. Indeed, from time to time its been more than a game with me as I've had numerous articles in *Pearsons Weekly, Tit Bits, Answers* and other mags on this hobby. I didn't get paid much for the articles. I did not expect much in cash but I got a wide correspondence and was able to meet up with fellow collectors and so 'swop' cards I didnt need for those I did need !

I must put on record the six sets of cards which I consider will ALWAYS be rare and always be worth £5 the set :

'British Medals and Decorations', issued by Taddy.

'Famous Actors and Actresses', issued by Taddy.

'Cricketers', issued in 1896 by Wills.

'Famous Authors and Poets', issued by Players (around 1896).

'Famous Explorers', issued by F. & J. Smith.

'Atlantic Liners', issued by Singleton & Cowe.

I would add a selection of Guinea Golds by Ogden and 'Rare and Interesting Stamps', a modern cigarette card set, and having got this little lot I'd give away 30,000 cards of mixed vintage. I believe (only I really shouldn't say so) I believe that only MINT fine complete sets of cigarette cards are any real *money* use and to have 30,000 bits and pieces is useless except to help others make their sets up. On this page is 39 years' experience in a nutshell.

Things to Come, a film I've just seen. 1937

If this is really things to come then I hope that I will be ever so dead long before they come. The only feature of this film is trick photography which is the best I've seen. It's a soulless film of a soulless world in which people like myself who are in no way mechanically minded would be quite lost. Unquestionably it *is* entertainment and yet honestly, diary, I wasn't entertained. I was fascinated and that's about all. I've said its soulless – perhaps that isn't quite the right word. It is devoid of warmth. It has no comfort. But we may never have another film like it – ever. One film like this is enough !

1938

Ever so late I've seen *The Scoundrel* which Charles MacArthur produced. It starts as if written by Oscar Wilde and ends rather more like Eugene O'Neill; the end breaks your blooming heart if films do break heart (which I doubt). Noël Coward is in this film and with due respect to him I wish that he wasn't for truly I *don't* think films is his medium, especially when we all know he has so many talents for other mediums. I don't think Mr Coward will *ever* make a film star because he is always Mr Coward. Now you cannot possibly say that of Clark Gable ! There's a very handsome lady in this film named, I believe, just 'Margo'. She has a very filmable face. And very dark flashing eyes. I would not like to put Margo out of temper ! Heck, for that matter nor would I care to displease Noël Coward – although his eyes *don't* flash.

The dialogue in *The Scoundrel* is a good deal crisper and tauter than we have been getting of late. It's *Not* one of those films that end happy-ever-after – but then you'd hardly expect it to do so with such a title ! Paid 1s. to see it – I WAS NOT Robbed.

September 1938

James Agate said something to me this week that I thought was rather clever – more so IF it was wit on the spur of the moment. He said 'The English always admire men of talent providing they are modest as well !' I thought to myself. My goodness, Look Who's talking about modesty. But of course I couldn't say that *to* him. He is so kind to me. . . Mr Agate looked very unwell – and he limped. Another over worked man. Another hurrying in the same way that Bennett hurried. Burning his candle at *every* end.

1938. Just a thought in passing

It strikes me that of all the actresses there are around, there is only one who isn't in my opinion STAGE STRUCK and for that matter has *never* been stage struck, and thats Gladys Cooper. Of course if I am wrong and shes ever likely to meet me, she is likely to strike me for saying so! But from what I see, to G. Cooper the stage is just a JOB. Often a very tiresome and boring job, but a job. One thing can be said for Miss G. Cooper : in the years Ive seen her around never never once, no matter what the weather, have I ever seen or heard her refuse to give an autograph, and bai jove thats really something. After all, she *is* SOMEONE (and jolly well knows it).

1939

H. G. Wells has said, 'A short story is a piece of writing which is short.'

Only a great literary man like Wells could put sound commonsense in such a concise manner. After all, a story is a piece of writing – just that ! If a chicken crosses the lane that is just an incident. But when, having crossed over, it finds a big worm and eats it, that's another incident following up, in sequence, and so makes a story.

1939

It is teatime and I am reading a book as Lizzie is cutting the brown bread. I say to her, 'I just cant get the hang of Einstein's Relativity.' And Lizzie says, 'Then why worry your head about it ? Give it back to him !'

1939

I learn with very amused interest that a lady in Ohio has just been granted a divorce. She told the judge that her husband had only spoken to her *three* times in the whole of their married life. She was granted the custody of the three children.

7th September 1940

I dont want war or blood and tears to creep into my journal ! Every army Colonel will write his memories (they always do). But something happened that must be recorded.

Lizzie had planned a picnic for us. We went to One Tree Hill, which is at the top of Peckham Park and one of the highest spots in South London. It was a glorious afternoon. Flowers were out. Trees were smiling and birds were singing. It couldn't have been a nicer Saturday afternoon. All seemed peacefull and we two were happy.

Suddenly the air raid siren went. We didn't move. Where could we go ? We were on top of a hill and there wasn't any shelter anywhere near us and in any case it was all of one hundred tall, wide steps to get down to the roadway and poor dear Lizzie has a bad heart and it had taken her near an hour to get *up* the hill with many halts en route. Suddenly a large number of enemy airplanes came over our heads – yes, right above us – and were intercepted by our planes and there was a fierce battle. Then came a terrific barrage from nearby guns and shrapnel fell almost like rain. It simply pattered down ! We could hear it falling and then several bombs fell nearby and the ground around us shook. I had with me a large loose raincoat. I put it over our heads, just as if it was raining light rain instead of deathly shrapnel and bombs ! And under that raincoat we continued our picnic. And somehow or another under that thin raincoat we felt quite safe ! And neither of us got injured. The Gods were kind to us. The things one does in wartime !

(All of a thousand houses were blitzed in London that afternoon and when the enemy returned that night *our* home was blitzed.)

Written at 2 in the morning, May 1941

Incendary bombs fell on my home this awfull night and have destroyed many thousands of my choicest cards, autographs and very personal souveniers. Isnt it odd. The German cards Nalda, the German girl, helped me to gather together in Germany two days before this bloody war started have now *all* been destroyed by a German bomb ! That must be *real* fate. Those bombs certainly had my name on them ! The fireman anxious to put out the blaze swamped the whole house with water. Huge big hoses gushing out water that wrecked my fragile treasures. I stood and cried. Yes, I cried. 25 years to collect items with loving care and less than 10 minutes to ruin so many of them.

I am myself very ill and my nerve is wrecked. I haven't

had a decent nights sleep for at least 2 weeks. Lizzie's home is also badly damaged. Her bed, some furniture and a good deal of her clothes are ruined. She is a wonderful treasure. You could see she was upset but she didn't break down. I was the one who broke down. Hell, this bloody war. Only one house in this road damaged this day ! OURS ! 152. *Sure* those bombs had my name on them. Ain't it strange ? German bombs to destroy German cards. If I could laugh I would laugh. Only I am not the stuff heroes are made of – so I cried.

I feel better now and we are going to have some wiskey and then try to get some of the water out of the basement. Its no use trying to dry out my treasures. The muck from fallen ceilings has made them quite useless. I wonder what has happened to Nalda. I hope *our* bombs dont kill her ! That would be *terrible* !

Some Ancient Remedies. (*Written in the middle of a Raid*)

Let us forget Hitler – the war – and even the problems of ration coupons for a while as I turn back the pages of the past for your amusement.

I stress amusement because, although I don't suppose any of them would do you the slightest harm, I have no wish for you to try them and then for some reason sue me because they don't now work! I don't suppose for one moment you would wish to roast the bones of a lambs head to ashes, mix those ashes to a paste with rose water and plaster and put it upon your jaw when you had the jaw ache ! The book, published in 1695, says 'this is a remedy which never fails to ease the pain.' I've no wish for you to write saying 'Dear Mr Bason your receipe for a potion to win my heart's desire hasn't worked,' but here is the potion. It consists of the heads of camomile flowers, a quart of the best claret wine, a liberal dash of wiskey plus the juice of langdebeet that has been gathered in June or July. 'Mix all together well and give unto thy love a glassfull two or three times a day and he will be thine for ever.' (I should jolly well think so !) The lady who gave this advice in 1798 knew a thing or two !

In *The Complete Herbel* by Culpeper, printed in 1653, there is an interesting receipt : Bawn water distilled in May restores the memory, quickens all the senses, strengthens the brain, the heart and the stomach, 'causes a merry wind' and a sweet breath. Well, well ! I must certainly find out what Bawn water is. It spells 'Whoopee' to me.

In *The Complete Gentlewoman*, printed in 1711, there is a very curious remedy – a cure for the bite of a mad dog. Write on a piece of paper these words:— REBUS – RUBUS – EPITEPSCUM : and give this to the party bitten to eat in bread. 'This never fails,' wrote Hannah Wooley round about 1710.

Overheard in Foyles, March 1942

'Although I'm married, I still like to take Romances to bed with me. They last longer than my old man !'

October 1942

The famous actress Marie Tempest is dead. She was the cause of the first (I think) appearance of me in print. I couldn't have been more than fourteen. She was in a play and several of us wanted her autograph after the first night. But she held in her arms a bunch of expensive flowers. I volunteered to hold the flowers whilst she signed our books, and she allowed me to do so. Alas, by the time she got to my book some one's pen had almost run dry and I got an autograph that was unreadable. (She replaced it eight years later.) However, in the gossip column of the *Evening News* the next night, it spoke of the play and of the reception and it said at the end 'one little chap had the proud privilege of holding Miss Tempest's bouquet whilst she signed autographs'. It failed to add that when I asked for a flower as a souvenir she said 'Most certainly *not*' – and got into her car without more ado !

A Bad time in my life. 1942

I've now been a week in The Red Cross Hospital at Tring. I feel a nervous wreck. They say I am likely to be here 'some months'. A very foolish doctor suggested yesterday I'd improve with *all* my teeth out ! I told him I'd much rather die than face a sadist dentist – and in any case my nerve has gone. My one hold on life is my Diary. Although days follow days and most of the days I am crying – although I cannot tell you why – and I am unable to speak clearly and seem to find trouble in forming words – yet I keep on writing and the Commandant says it is alright. She is a very tough stout solid woman, in uniform with a row of medal ribbons. She has very rosy cheeks but she is *not* matronly or 'motherly'. She is hard – but just. She calls me 'a highly strung individual.' I dont like this 'individual' business but can say nothing.

The food is good and theres plenty. In a barn 100 yards from the hospital there is an old grand piano and I play a little on it each day. Its long years since my mother gave me a piano for my 21st birthday and sold it whilest I was out at work just a day or so after I was 22 ! I never forgave her this petty nasty business. She sold it for six pounds and had her hair dyed WHITE and beautifully permed in Bond St. on the proceeds ! Its pleasant to try to remember tunes. My mind wont work on *whole* tunes but I get bits and pieces.

I have my name and the hospital address tied on to my buttonhole with a luggage label. I'm a parcel going nowhere ! My mother visited me yesterday and it was most unpleasant. She knew of my unnatural fear of dentists yet was such a cow as to stress her advice to have all my teeth out. She made me cry. I ran away from her.

I told Nurse Robinson I did *not* want my mother ever to call again.

Lizzie will come next week. I am allowed *one* visitor a week. I am allowed out (with company) of hospital 2 hours a week. I am forbidden to go out alone, but I do not want to go out at all. My fractured leg (Potts Fracture) is pain because I have plaster blisters which itch. I am very unhappy. I must hold on – to what – to whom ? To Nurse Robinson ? She's a 'stunner' – and at eleven stone could stun me any time of day or night.

1945

Long years ago Arnold Bennett told me of a time when he wrote a letter to a newspaper which had attacked him and his then latest novel (probably *Lord Raingo*). He had completed the letter when the phone rang and his secretary told him that the *same* paper was asking for a short article by him, so he crossed out Dear Sir and Yours Truly and had it retyped and sold it to them for 'a goodly sum'.

I mention this because I was asked this week to talk on books to a posh ladies club. I was very very willing to do this talk for nothing. However, Lizzie said only fools talk for nothing and *made* me go to a phone and ask 'How much ?' The voice at the other end told me to wait. 5 minutes dead silence and then the decision. 5 gns. and a good meal afterwards. There is a moral. I will not talk for nothing *ever again* ! Lizzie is a treasure. She curbs my impulsiveness. Dr Johnson said 'Only a fool writes for nothing.' Now I say only a fool talks for nothing but it took wise Lizzie to make me see it !

August 1946

One of the results of contributing to *The Saturday Book* (I am in volume 5) is the wide mail it brings from a variety of people. Four days ago I had a letter from a clergyman in Scotland and he wanted a copy of *The Sacred Flame*, a play by Maugham. It was unfortunate that I didn't have a copy – and a quick glance around other people's libraries did not bring one to light so I sent him a list of books that I did have and wanted to sell. By return post I got an order with cash and he purchased A Flemish-English 2-way Dictionary, a not very nice book on flagellation that I was pleased to see the back of and a fine copy of *The Doll* by L. A. G. Strong.

Now I wonder what this clergyman is *really* like! There seems no companionship between any of the 3 books and if you add *The Sacred Flame* the gaps widen even more. Why does a man – any man – suddenly buy a Flemish Dictionary from a stray list? Why, except for sheer morbid curiosity, does a Vicar want a book on flogging? Of course *The Doll* is a great short story and anyone would buy that.

Its always been a mystery to me the type of books my clients buy. I know why *I* buy them – but I do often wonder why others buy them. There is a really Victorian lady up in Harrogate who buys the grimest and toughest of gangster tales – and yet to see her you'd think she'd think *Vanity Fair* ever so fast and furious and Marie Correlli very forward. And there's a doctor who only buys books on ropes, knotes and kindred subjects. I've often wondered why, and rather afraid to ask him. And a meek little man who only collects books on fungus and mushrooms with illustrations – yet he works in a bank, lives in Streatham and only has a small unpretentious little garden without even one tree. Why mushrooms and eatable fungus! Oh, its just a hobby – one must collect *something*!

Have I ever recorded Mr B. in Chicago who collected chamber pots? Yes sir, thats all he collected; had dozens of them, some in solid *silver*. I sold Mr B. a lovely catalogue with a full range of pots in it. He was delighted –

so delighted that he sent me a signed photo of a Chicago stripteaser and it was autographed by her in a most extraordinary place and manner ! A Mayor who looked *so* pious bought that ! The world of collecting is indeed a most pleasant world.

1946

Make no mistake *Brief Encounter* is a real honey of a film – pure cinema and real life – the material which *makes* life. Its well acted, superbly produced and magnificently directed. The story is by Noël Coward. Its the best British picture I've seen in years – and it will live years in my memory. Lizzie had a good cry over this film. . . and indeed lots of folks were crying – with genuine emotion. The dialogue is superb and crisp. Yes *Brief Encounter* is superb – and I have to particularly mention Joyce Carey, Trevor Howard, Celia Johnson, Stanley Holloway and Margaret Barton from the cast. Directed by David Lean. Produced by N.C. and I would say at a guess he did *all* the dialogue.

1946

I mentioned in an article I wrote for a Norman Kark publication that I was single. I didn't do it for any reason, just as a statement of fact. 3 weeks later (yesterday) I got such a nice letter from a lady over Shepherds Bush-way. She would love to meet me for she'd enjoyed my writings. I suggested we met at 7 at Lyons in Coventry Street. I told her what I'd be wearing and exactly where I would be standing. And to help matters, I would carry a copy of *Tit-Bits*. I was there on time. She arrived very soon afterwards – with her MOTHER, her father and her brother ! I said 'Blimey ! Why the party ?' She said 'Surely you didn't expect me to come here to the West End to meet a strange man *unprotected* ?'

1946

Oh isnt it *wonderfull* ! A man got Free Legal aid by making some false statements as to his income. He was then summoned and he elected to have free legal aid to fight this case – and got it. I do hope he won that case. I so often see first class tales in newspapers but only the *beginning* of them. Now I shall never know if the free legal aid got him off the free legal aid case !

Grand National Night, 1947

Heaven protect little me. A female woman has sent me her typed MSS. novel. It is called 'This Age of Misery'. Its a huge novel – at a very rough guess between 180,000 and 200,000 words. Will I read it ? Will I touch it up here and there ? Will I try to sell it for her on, say, 20% commission ? (Commission of *what* ?) I am miserable enough today without this bloody thankless hopeless task. I had 2s. on a horse today which did *not* win the Grand National. Indeed the blooming horse fell at the 2nd hurdle. I wish they'd BAN The Grand National. I wish I could ban wouldbe authors sending me quite unasked their work. It will cost me two shillings to return 'This Age of Misery'. If that woman was here right now I'd touch *her* up – by golly I would. 'This Age of Misery'. What a Bloody Title. It's dead before it starts it's rounds. I will tell her that – not that she'll take *any* notice. It isn't as if I'm a novelist ! Will I touch it up ? Well, fancy that !

In Tower Bridge Road, Bermondsey, 1947

There is not any trade. I have sat beside my book barrow for the past hour and taken ninepence – 3d. for some comics and sixpence for *Kitty*, a novel by Warwick Deeping. I have been reading Alexander Pope and I bet as how I am the only person in Bermondsey, indeed in the whole of South London, who is dipping into Pope this black morning. I've come upon a passage which seems to fit the occasion. It is this : To endeavour to work upon the vulgar with a fine sense is like attempting to hew rocks with a razor.

On my stall I have books by T.S. Eliot, Maugham, Drinkwater and A. Huxley. They are good books and they are priced at 1s. 6d. or less a copy. Many I myself paid more for than the price I ask ! But they do not sell in Bermondsey. Yet, if I put upon my stall a paper jacket book of trash with a picture of a well busted tart on the cover and titled *Love for Sale* it would sell. I cannot tell why that is so when for the most part even the buyers *know* they will read trash and that there will be a few rapes and some bald words and thats about *all*. Do men get a bit of a thrill from reading these Books ? I never did. But when Ive been forced to sell these awfull books (or never pay my way) its been mostly women of over 45 who have been the eager buyers ! Is it their way to recapture the romances which have passed ? I asked a woman only once and she pretty nearly slapped my face. So the writings of Eliot and the rest remain unsold and I sit here getting cold – with A. Pope on my lap. Maybe I should have A. Trollope on my lap ! COR–APUN ! !

On Mozart, 1947

My kind landlady Lizzie is my greatest treasure. A source of good clean fun. She never went to school – but is an expert housekeeper and a very wonderfull lady. Sort of Johnson to my Boswell.

I tried to talk music one night and I opened the conversation with this. Do you like Mozart ? She thought awhile and then said, 'Aint that what Italians do on the walls of churches ?'

October 1947

Today I popped into Constables the publishers and had a pleasant 30 minutes chat with amiable Michael Sadleir.

I had the good luck to sell him some 50 or 60 tissue paper souveniers of events of the last 50 years. I asked him fifty shilling and saying that it was very cheap he paid cash at once. He said he didnt know what on earth he was going to do with them. I was not able to tell him! All that mattered to me was that I'd made 10s. profit. He also autographed for me his Novel called *Priviledge*. I am glad Mr Sadleir didnt ask me if I'd read it because I had *not* – and I didn't intend to do so either! I had a client in USA wanting that Novel. Why should I soil a new copy with a free read?

Mr Sadleir was in a chatty mood and he told me that he knows a man who collects BACK COLLAR STUDS. Yes thats *all* he collects – back studs. When he comes upon one of the 1860 period brown with age and looking like old ivory he is really delighted. Well I was then forced to tell Michael of a bloke I know who collects Toilet papers. Yes, toilet paper and he has specimens pasted into albums with the details of what W.C. it came from beneath the paper (*un*used of course! !). This bloke has Royal W.C. paper Monogramed and all. Mr Sadleir did laugh – and as usual we parted very good friends. M.S. has a *grand* sense of humour. Once again he gave me too much gin to drink – insisting that it put hairs on my chest. For 4th or 5th time in 25 years I arrived home slightly tight.

I once met money (*written 1948*)

A chap called Smell has just gone. He is an American and wanted vols 1, 3 and 4 of *The Saturday Book*. I was able to provide 3 and 4 but I could not let my first volume go in case I am not able to get another, whereas I have vols 3 and 4 six times over. When he said, 'I'm Smell' it took all manners to ask if he *did*. But he didnt smell, his money had a nice *fresh* smell. It occured to me, Diary, that I shouldn't say anything about odd names when my own is so odd. At school I was nicknamed Pudding – 'Pudding' Basin.

Ive never regretted my odd name and I dont suppose Smell does either. But Ive never yet written about the time in a Surrey lane I met MONEY. It was a wet surface and I was on my old bike and not looking where I was going and I skidded badly and fell off of my bike. A middle aged man (who looked the double of Mussolini) was passing by and came to my side and asked if I was hurt. I was not hurt but I was a little shaken up. He advised me to rest under a tree out of the rain untill I got my breath back. I put my bike under the tree and he stood beside me. Who are you, he asked. Whats your name ? How do you make your living ? He seemed rather lonely – like as if he wanted a little chat and I was very willing to chat – if only to get my mind off the bump I'd gone on that hard roadway. I told him my name and that I sold Books for my living.

'How interesting. A noble proffesion. Keep to it. Books are friendly things. Have you heard of the Encloypedia Brittanica ?'

'Oh yes, sir, I've heard of it but its out of my line of business. My clients only want Brawn and Busts – novels of action or sex. They dont want education. I couldnt sell that Brittanica even for a quid, not even if I put in a pound of tea as well.'

He laughed and called me a funny lad. Then he said, 'I'm Money.'

'Well sir,' I said, 'if you are *Money* I would like a bit of you. I'm in need of money ! How can I get some ?'

He pondered a moment and then said 'With *your* Brains and *other* peoples Brawn. . . Dont work hard. Work *wisely*. And when money eventually is yours and it will be – it WILL BE – then let your money work for you as you sit back and enjoy life and read good books – including the Enclopedia Brittanica. Goodbye.' And having delivered that mouthfull of wisdom he departed with a friendly tap on my shoulder.

I stood under that tree ten minutes doing nothing at all and then just as I was readjusting my handle bars, which had got out of shape, a policeman also on a bike passed by. Then he returned on his bike and asked if anything was wrong ? I said No – nothing was wrong except that I'd fallen off my bike. I then said that although there was nothing wrong with me there was probably something wrong with the old man who'd just gone up the road. He was probably round the Bend. He said that he was MONEY. The policeman seemed very amused. He'd just passed him. He knew him well by sight. Looks like Mussolini ? Yes thats him. Called himself Money.

'He had every right to call himself Money for he *is* Money. His name is Sir Leo Money !' And with that he departed.

I thought the policeman was kiddin me. But I put down the name. When I was able two or 3 days later I went to Southwark Public Library Reference Room and looked him up (Money *not* the policeman) and there was such a man and quite a big pot !

As I write this now in 1948 I dont know if Sir Leo is still alive. But I do know he gave me a Basonfull of wisdom that afternoon in a Surrey lane. I'd never forgotten it although Ive not been able to put it much practical purpose. I've never had Money – but at least I once *saw* Money !

Fan Mail from the Gold Coast (exact copy), January 1948

Dear Unknown friend,

In reading a certain Book called A'SAT BOOK I came across your lovely article and address I am the stamps collector in Gold Coast, and I want to keep a lovely friend with you.

I am very glad when I have got your Lovely Name and the address. Please try to send me a photograph of yourself and the S A T C addresses Book. In few days ago I have sick very Bad, so that I can't send you any stamps in my first letter. But I will try to send you more stamps in my next letter Kindly reply Me a soon as you receive this letter. I waiting to you.

Yours faithfully friend

ENOCH K. ODOI

My reply :

Dear Enoch,

Its nice to know that you've enjoyed my work in *The Saturday Book* and I hope you will like my future work in it. I cant write a long reply as I have so much to do but I do appreciate a letter from you. Good Luck !

I am very friendly

FRED BASON

P.S. I enclose some English stamps as a gift.

More fan mail from the Gold Coast. January 1948

I did not ever expect to hear again as I hadn't enclosed a photo of Lovely Me nor did I know (or care) what 'S A T C addresses Book' ment ! But blessed are those who expect so little because I *did* get a reply – only the astounding thing was it came from an entirely different person – or at least with a much changed name. Enoch was no more. Now we had a letter from Mr Jacob A. Annan. Such a nice letter. Here it is :

Mr Bason,

I received your letter with GREAT thanks. I know you have No time to write ME; but yet, as a friend you will get little chance to write ME. As you said you dont like Gold Coast News, I think it best to avoid mentioning to you. I hope Casablanca is a very fund place of enjoyment. It is a mistake for me to use you name Like that. I creat pardon. Give me some hints about the Boxing of Tommy and Braddock. As for Joe Louise he is well known to be a good Boxer. I will *not* send you Newspapers as you do not read them. I have collect cigarette cards I want to send them to you. Did you like them ? Please dont take our school address always take this New address Accra. Earthquake ocured in Gold Coast damage houses and killed people. We are not well in our town we sleep in tents and playgrounds, because every time He occured. And if *you* live in your house and he occured you will DIE. You dont know whether your house will be Break and fell unto you. So we dont sleep or live in our houses. I am learning my lessons. Best compliments to you. Urgent reply Please.

Yours sincerely

JACOB A. ANNAN

In the face of such a letter I could do nothing else but reply – be it only for the sake of international Good Will ! You could see that Mr Annan had laboured most carefully over his air mail letter to me and although I could make slightly less heads than tails out of it I felt bound to answer his letter, and this is what I wrote :

Dear Jacob Annan,

I do not know what has happened to Enoch – probably the earth quake has accounted for him. I was pleased to hear from you. As you guessed I have no great interest in Gold Coast news because by the time it reaches me it has turned into History – and I have never been keen on History. I am keen on Boxing. By 'Tommy' I am sure you mean Tommy Farr and I think that he is an outstanding heavyweight and we are most proud of him in England. Mr Braddock is as you know an American and I have not seen him fight – but people who have watched him consider that Tommy Farr is all round the better boxer, with a better left hand – and as thats the hand which I consider *really* matters in my opinion Mr Farr will beat Mr Braddock on any occasion they may meet.

I *do* collect cigarette cards and will be most happy to send you nice foreign stamps in fair exchange for your cards (which please pack carefully as bent soiled old dirty cards are USELESS to me).

I am sorry you are not well in your town but there is nothing whatever I can do about that. Keep on learning your lessons. And learn to use a straight left in your boxing, then very likely you will become a boxing champion and earn lots of money and will then be able to make your town all well again. Good luck to you.

Very truly

FRED BASON

I never heard again. In the past 10 years Ive never had another letter from the Gold Coast.

1948

I've been going pretty well once a week to the cinema since I was 8. At 8 I paid ONE penny each Saturday for my seat. In 1948 its a trifle more but on the whole I do *not* begrudge the encrease in price as film stars cost more now and so does Alimoney. Looking back I could, I suppose name 12 outstanding films that I could see again. I really never had a favourite film star of either sex (or in between) because theres parts of so many I've greatly enjoyed. Its the same with films. Today I can list at last – at long last, my *favourite* film, the film in which everyone was great and every bit of photography was superb. The story was impressive and I sat spell bound by superb entertainment. The film is *The Treasure of Sierra Madre*. It stars Mr H. Bogart – but everyone in this film is a star and the brigands with minor parts are superb. I would willingly pay 5s. to see it again. In my childhood I liked *Treasure Island* and *King Solomons Mines*. Maybe there is a romantic line in me that the rubber of time hasn't erased. To think these men in the film sweated their guts out for gold-dust – and in the end it blew away in the wind in one of the most dramatic settings and finest endings I've *ever* seen.

Two great films in two years. Charlie Chaplin in *Monsieur V* and now Bogart at his toughest – The Man You Love to Hate !

I haven't the autograph of either which I must try to remedy some day – and yet why bother such stars, why trouble them ? I should only be one more 'worry' and I wouldn't like that. I forget who wrote *Sierra Madre* but he's a gold mine of a writer. I wish I was a 1/10th as good.

Oh to be in Mexico NOW, seeking treasure. Writing is work ; this week I've worked hard. I need a change. . . and I desperately need a wife. She'd be my treasure just as long as she never gets the illusion that authors are lazy.

29th August 1948

Today is my Birthday and dear Lizzie gave me two winter shirts as a present. It was the only present I had. I don't regret the passing of the years. True, they seem to go faster and faster each passing year but each one is more interesting. I get more mail each year and never fail to answer every letter. It keeps me poor but it keeps my readers happy (I hope). I always said to myself that if I ever got fan mail I would answer it faithfully, fully and truthfully as soon as possible after its arrival and I've kept that promise.

I suppose that now I can claim (not that I want to do so) that I am known all over the world – except in Burma, Russia and Poland – from every other country I've seemed to have had mail since I started this writing game. 16 people in Fiji know me. Eleven people in the furthest part of Northern Canada write often. In the Indian Ocean there is an isolated island but on it the governor knows me. I get a stream of letters from Australia and I've even had letters from Iceland and Greenland. But I've never had a letter from my own district of Southwark ! A bloke has no honour at all on his own home ground. . .

I am reminded of what Arnold Bennett told me. 'You will never get praise from your nearest or dearest.' He said he pretty nearly broke his heart when with pride he displayed his first published novel to a close relation and got a cold reception.

In this life one needs *fortitude* ! My private life is terribly lonely. My public life is a mass of chance acquaintances, casual friendships and much mail. If this is fame then its EMPTY.

1948

I have chatted with an Indian from Bombay (*not* a Red Indian from USA – that's a treat for the future). This coloured gentleman considers that the English are very unclean people because we wear the same shoes that we walked about in the streets with when we enter our homes ! He also said he had seen English children playing on the floors made unclean by the dust and germs of those outdoor shoes worn indoors. He said, on entering any house – your own or any one elses – you should take off your shoes in the hall and put on slippers !

Do you know this has never never occured to me. When at times I don slippers it is only to rest my feet and not for any higenic reasons. I know the Chinese do this changing of footwear – but they are strange people at the best of times. It would have been a most convincing conversation if the Indian had not had a body odour that was a really unpleasant smell !

January 1949

I had a letter from Reg today. It took me near two hours to go through a pile of old mail seeking 'Reg'. Oh, I do wish to Goodness people would use an atom of common sense – Reginald is not all that uncommon. Why couldn't he put *both* his names ?

I find at last I'd got him on file. Such a kind bloke. He helped me out when in a noble war effort I spent 2 weeks in 1942 on a Hertfordshire farm. It was all so fresh to me and I am afraid I neglected to do my allotted tasks. I earnt 13s. for a weeks work ! And I mean *work*. I was doing it all far too slow to make even my expenses. Reg Davies came to my rescue. He did his work and then mine as well. He was an experienced hand at farm work. I was happy to give him my wages. He was a joy amongst companions. A jolly worker and a happy man. He also needed the money a great deal more than I did.

Now 8 years later he writes again. He is hard up and is sending some books in hope I will buy them. The parcel arrives. I've never seen such JUNK ! But I send him a pound note. The world is a nicer place for having men like Reg Davies in it. He will probably always be broke or near broke but what matter – the income tax treasury swines will not be able to take blood from *his* stone !

I best say that whilest Reg did my farm work I laid behind a hay stack reading *Decline and Fall*. . .Another week of farm work and I'd have fallen into a decline !

Down My Road. 9th April 1949

Mrs Hendries of Southwark Borough Council said at a Council meeting last week (and I have it from the local press in black and white) that the Westmoreland Rd. district was like a Black Hole of Calcutta and they were frequently hearing of people being assaulted in the dark down there. She did not say who 'they' were. She said the district was getting a bad name. Why not have every light on in the Walworth Rd. and more lights in the side streets ? Mr Caldwell of the same Council said it was the Council's policy to keep the main roads well lighted all night but the lights in the side streets went out at midnight. He (Mr Caldwell) said 'I suggest there is *nothing* low or terrible about the Westmoreland Rd.'

Well, I agree with Mr Caldwell (whoever he happens to be) for I've lived 40 years in this said socalled dangerous road and never found it terrible. I would hate to have to tell my rich American admirers that they will need a body guard when they visit me ! As long as you mind your own business and 'keep your nose clean' and *out* of other people's affairs Walworth is safe. You must NEVER prevent or stop a fight. You never take sides. You don't 'nark' on other people and then everything is roses – be it light or dark in my road.

My Mother (written 1949)

In 1930 without telling my folks about it I wrote a book, found a publisher and in 1931 it was published in a flaming red cloth with gilt designs. The publisher gave me 6 copies and with great joy and much personal pride I took them home and up to my attic. There, having gloated over them for the best part of an hour I took one copy downstairs and displayed it to my Mother.

'Look, mum,' I said, 'I am a *real* author ! Here is a book all by me – and its got my name on the cover *and* inside as well.' She was doing some needlework at the time and she glanced up from her work and said,

'A book ! Well, put the bloody thing down – and run and get me half a pint of milk at once. Theres sixpence on the dresser.'

I went and got the milk at the local dairy and felt that whilest I was away she'd have time to look at her only son's *first* book ! When I returned she made me go into the yard and fill a scuttle of coal. As I went out to get it I noticed that my book was still in the same place by her side of the table and had not been touched. It took me more than a quarter of an hour to get the coal and when

I again returned to the kitchen my book was *still* unopened. I took up my book from the table and took it up again to my attic and put it with the other five copies and then I lay on my bed and *cried.* I never forgave my mother. An author so desperately needs a pat on the back !

18th October 1949

It seems to me very nearly impossible to access the pleasure other people get out of life or of their own way of living. I've known in my time some remarkably rich people and for the most part I didn't find them uncommonly happy. Indeed, some seemed happy being miserable or got their pleasures by making others miserable. I have known poor people who's eyes reflected the genuine happiness they got from life. They have a smile and a cheerfull word for everyone. You seldom see them angry or wearing frowns and yet you know they are extremely poor people. Money or the lack of it doesn't seem to really trouble them.

I've been awfully hard up from time to time and when I've been hungry I've been bloody miserable and full of self pity and felt that the world owed me a slim living. But I know a chap in Hastings who I'm positive hasn't £1 in all the world and wouldnt know where to borrow a pound. He has in a kit bag 4 tooth combs, 2 ordinary combs, several books, washing utensils and a pair of socks and 3 white collars. I am pretty positive he hasn't got anything else – oh, except, maybe, 10s. or 12s. but he is happy. He will travel the whole of the South coast dish washing and sleeping rough. He will work for his food and maybe a few bob over. He's 46. He has no home and no relations. He is ever so happy ! I don't believe a really rich man could be happier. I was proud and happy to meet him. We had a long chat. He is ever so wise. He says 'possessions are a hindrance to adventure.'

On the other hand there is Lady T. out in Switzerland. Recently she complained to me about the rate of exchange, the price of *The Saturday Book*, the servant problem, the weather, the prospects of a 3rd War and the low class of visitors from England to Switzerland all in *one* letter ! I know her to be quite rich. I know her now to be a miserable old bitch and I want no part of her. If you want to let off steam and have a bloody good moan surely you can do it on your own doorstep – or like me keep a journal and get it out of your system by writing it all down.

I've a strange idea that with all his fame and fortune Ivor Novello is not a particularly happy man. I've an even stronger idea that the astounding and remarkable Aldous Huxley is also none too happy. Right at the top of the tree – surely all their dreams have come true ! When a man has one million pounds it seems he wants another to keep it company. I do not understand this at all. I never shall ! I know a Welsh Novelist who rubs along on less than 150 pounds a year. I've never once seen him miserable or at cross purposes with the world. I believe its something within one, some part of one's make up, some gland that causes happiness and it has nothing to do with fame or fortune.

I can't in truth say that I am always happy. I keep seeking – and at times I don't know what I seek. If I knew that though I'd be happier. And it ain't religion either, for I've known some remarkably miserable Vicars ! It ain't sex. Many tarts are happy women !

Oh, it's so strange – people I mean. 'Nothing is stranger than people and their moods.' Sax Rohmer wrote this (in red ink) to me years ago. The older I get the more I agree with his mouth-full. But I do believe that faith in a God *does* help. I often feel less restless after saying simple prayers. I learnt to pray when some swines in the civil service were making my life utter hell. Prayer alone kept me from killing myself. There is *power* in prayer !

3rd January 1950

Two days ago at Streatham there died Kate Carney, and a large slice of real old London has gone. She was the real Coster Queen, the exuberant Cockney. There was no one and there never will be again another Kate Carney for her London is fast disappearing. She could hold her audience with that sad song 'Are we to part like this, Bill ?' or get 'em laughing and joining in with '3 Pots a Shilling,' and *no one* else could !

Her songs were almost tailor made for her. She made them her own and for 63 years she was a star of the GENUINE music hall. Indeed, she was singing ballads in Victorian days – and so she was a star through 5 reigns. She was a big fat plain looking woman with a big chest and a large heart. She was ALL big and there wasn't anything mean about her. She had a loud voice and loud ways – but she was a real dear old girl. She lived most of her life in Brixton and her home was like as if nothing had been changed in it for 40 years. It was all Edwardian and stout. Even the piano was of the 1912 period with fretwork front inlaid with mother of pearl.

She must have appeared in many Royal Command Performances in her time. I understand she started on the Halls at Collins in Islington, and was friends with Marie Lloyd. Kate Carney was always larger than life. Her husband was George Barclay who owned a music hall at Stoke Newington called The Alexandra. I've never been there. They must have been married all of 40 years. He died in 1945 and we thought Kate Carney would retire – but not a bit of it. You couldn't keep Kate down – not that you'd want to.

I got her autograph first in 1922 (the same year as I got Marie Lloyds). She was fat in 1922. She was still fat in 1942. In between those 20 years I'd seen her 5 times in almost the same act – and the same resonant voice. She never needed a microphone. Her dress was coster in every way and her hat a blaze of Happy Hampstead feathers. She was a REAL Cockney – everyone said that. But when I asks her where she was born she said it was a question she did not like to answer ! I have often wondered if she adopted London. She was a ballad singer at 16 and a ballad singer at 76. She died at 80 – and *never* retired ! For last year 1949 she was still singing 'Are we to part like this, Bill ?' She was at Southend in the music hall there and a huge success (at 79).

Its like I've said, a piece of real old Cockney London is gone and I'm down right sorry. I believe she had children. Will one of them carry on the tradition ? I expect not. What's gone is gone forever !

1950

I often wondered why Ray Robinson the great boxer was called 'Sugar'. The time I saw him fight he didn't look a bit sweet, indeed, he looked fierce. Then I learnt that Mr Robinson received nearly £9,000 for knocking out Mr Van Dam in 13 minutes in 1950. Thats about seven hundred pounds per MINUTE ! Sugar in any language. Sweet by *any* standard. So no wonder he is called 'Sugar'.

Said to have been heard in a bookshop, 1950

'Have you Dickens' unfinished *Edwin Drood* ?'

'Oh No, Madam, all our books are complete ! !'

November 1950

I think that I had better make some comment in my diary once about the fearfull monster (as some folks call it) called Television. Publishers and cinema folks seem to fear it. I dont fear it at all, although its not a medium I am fond of as it makes one too wellknown by sight.

I am very sorry for the very silly people who sit with their eyes glued to screens for hours after hours. They are darft. Soon they will lose the gentle art of conversation, and thats a very noble art. Soon they will miss very interesting novels and astounding short stories. Soon they will miss the wonderfull smell and spell of a real theatre and flesh and blood actors and actress, and the thrill of a first night. Soon they will lose the wonderfull joys of family life, as they sit like stuffed dummies before a screen being dolled out things by so called experts and lapping it up as if it was facts. Television will even kill romance. Oh I know its mostly seen in the dark, and many a romance breeds in the dark, but lovers holding hands want to speak sweet nothings – which mean so very much – and they cannot do that when the telly is on.

I would far sooner see a pair of flashing eyes than a flashing screen. And if strip tease ever comes to TV it will not amuse me. Even a love scene seems secondhand on TV. For myself I would sooner a seat in Regents Palace Hotel alone and have a drink and watch the passers-by than watch an hour of TV. Bai jove, soon people won't know the joys of a walk in the park, or of watching boys sail ships on a lake. They wont be able to recognise the songs of birds, only the songs of Vera Lynn ! They sit and stare at Muggeridge and they lap it all up. I would for my part far far sooner have loving arms around a nice lady in a park, on cool grass, far far away from TV, than ANY programme Ive yet seen.

And for the winter evenings a glass of whiskey, my pipe and very good novel and you can keep TV ! It certainly won't ever keep me, and I believe that inside ten years sensible people will have it only in very small doses. Right now its still a big novelty, but oh, how sorry I am for the silly people who now spend six hours every night of the week watching it. It's like a drug, indeed it *is* a drug. Give me a book, or a nice conversation, and you can keep

TV. Mark you, I may change me mind later on, but I hope not.

4th January 1951

I don't often record things to do with illness, not even my own. Bennett and Agate did enough of that. But today I heard a rather astounding thing. There was a girl who went to a doctor because she had stomach pains. The doctor thought it might be appendix trouble, so the girl has an operation for appendix and out it came. But several months later she again has severe pains and went to same doctor. He said 'Well, it cannot be appendix,' so he gave her some soothing tummy medicine. He got talking to her, for she was a very pretty girl of nineteen – note nineteen. He found out that she knew none of the facts of life at all, and that honestly she thought she could become pregnant by being kissed on the lips. She had been kissed, several times, mostly against her will, and every time she had been kissed, the severe stomach pains commenced. The doctor told her, there and then in rough and ready language, the entire facts of life and just how babies arrive. He said that he did it to ease the girl's state of mind. She had not been to him since – and never had the pains again. Isn't the mind a strange thing ? I am assured this is true and happened quite recently in Stockport !

January 1951

Oh doesn't it break ones blooming heart. A comedian asked me to write a monologue suitable for stag parties and cabaret work. I oblige sometimes with this sort of job because it amuses me and I came up with a smashing one called 'Spicy Sue' – who knew *just* what to do. I asked a small sum of 50s. for it outright, so it could be his exclusive monologue. He has now turned it down because he requires something *historical* ! Personally, I would have said the more hysterical the better ! Why on earth historical ? I will not write another for him. If I wrote one about Napoleon, I am sure the prospective client would say 'Oh no – it must be about Sabrina.' (Poor Sabrina. The latest joke I've heard about her is that her new house has two bay windows for obvious reasons !) If Billy Bennett was alive, he would buy 'Spicy Sue'. We lack down-to-earth comics now. Only Max Miller keeps the flag flying.

I do like a bit of earthy humour – like the man who refused to pay five pounds for a cup tie ticket. He said, 'I could get the best woman in London for £5.' And the ticket tout said, 'Maybe, but could you get her for an hour and a half, and the band of the Welsh Guards playing in the interval ?' Oh, how Arnold Bennett would have enjoyed this !

1951

I do not put much music in my diaries, but I do know the pieces I enjoy. One of my favourite pieces is Symphony No.3 in F by Brahms, and when I hear it I seem to get a feeling of happiness within me and its a tonic. I was listening to it on Sunday, February 4th, 1951. A bitterly cold and windy day. It didn't stop raining the whole day. We didn't have much coal and it was chilly at 152. When it was over I said to Lizzie that was Symphony No.3 in F. Just by way of conversation and she upped and said at once 'In furs I suppose !' It made me laugh. She had never heard of Brahms. But then I'll take six to four with anyone she has never heard of Mozart, Delius or Dvorak either ! But it doesnt do her any *harm*. It made the day brighter.

If I had my way I would have friends to tea each Sunday. For 20 years my At Home day has been (and still is) Thursdays – but the folks who call on Thursdays are mostly ships who will be passing in a night. They call to see Lizzie and me out of sheer curiosity. Sometimes I do believe they think they will find a resurrected James

Agate. I am ever sociable on Thursdays, but I like my close friends to tea on Sundays.

I must confess that I so seldom go to church or chapel these days. I found the sermons locally so very dull – and the churches themselves dull, and bleak and comfortless. Do I have to sit on a very hard upright uncomfortable seat in order to get close to God ? No, I dont think so. Nor do I have to listen to an uninspiring sermon mumbled away. No wonder the churches of Southwark are 3 parts empty ! And why are vicars for the most part so stuffy ? Religion is their living. Thats a fact. But if they got paid by results of souls *saved* they'd starve !

Still, this will *not* do. Ive made it a rule to avoid politics and religion in my diaries and here I am on religion. And we started with Brahms and finish with the Bible. Well thats variety at least !

1951

Today I had a letter from Herne Bay. It is from a girl of seventeen who asks for advice as she says I'm the 'most sensible author she's read' ! (What does she read ?) She wants to know whether it's best for her to remain at school another year or so or go out in the world now at seventeen and seek experience, because more than anything else in the world, she wants to become a novelist. I have replied, after some thought, that she'd best remain at school at least one more year because education is invaluable. I suggested that she devoted that year, if possible, to expert shorthand and typewriting, plus cookery and the arts of being female – gracious and charming and *a lady*. So that if her writing ever fails, she has many more irons in the fire. I suggested that equipped with secretarial scholarship, plus charm, she would soon be married and that's what *really* mattered. I hope the girl doesn't show the letter all round the school. But I found it quite difficult to advise her. She should have asked her dad – but at seventeen, I know what difficulty I found in asking my own father anything at all !

I have the most astounding mail a writer could get ! Remember the time, Diary, when I was asked to go over to Notting Hill to see if a girl of nineteen was safe and well ? Her mother in Cornwall was *worried* ! I was to look Miss Nineteen over and see if she was healthy and *clean* – and if she needed new *underclothes* ! I was to take her girl out and buy them and send her the bill – and in due course I would be paid. Just imagine me going up to a strange girl and saying 'Your mother says I've to see if your underclothes want replacing.' What bloody cheek, she would have said, and that's what I wrote to mum in Cornwall who knew I could be trusted ! Probably – but could I trust Miss 19 ? Was'nt worth the risk !

About Last Night. 29th September 1951

On September 28th 1951 I was Mr John Ford's guest at the Publishers Representatives Association Annual Guest Night. The previous year I had stood outside and watched the guests arrive and although I knew at least seventy of them, none spoke to me, and no one had invited me, so I protested in a column I was writing in a trade paper and Mr Ford promised that next year I would be his guest – and he kept his word (bless him).

Two things happened at this do that are worth recording. For the very first time I met John Hadfield who, in 1949, had written to say that he didn't believe I was alive and that he thought I was a figment of Leonard Russell's imagination. So now John knows for sure I *am* very much alive !

The second thing was that the Duke of Windsor was down to be the principle speaker. Now, I am not a one for royalty and all that sort of expensive luxury, but I had a sort of admiration for Edward, so looked forward to hearing him talk and seeing him for once in person. But he let the company down and did not turn up, making as his excuse the King's illness – although Princess Elizabeth and the Duke of Edinburgh attended the premiere of the Florence Nightingale picture the day before the operation on September 28th. The day the Duke of Windsor was to speak they were both at a race meeting and I say if Princess Elizabeth can attend a race meeting, the duke should have been able to have spoken at a small select gathering of Book Trade Representatives, especially as his book *A King's Story* was the feature of the 'do'. However, that is only a personal opinion and there were probably other factors that I do not know about which stopped the duke attending.

But sending Lord Beaverbrook's son instead to speak was a pleasant surprise (and a nice job he made of it – and he had such a nice personality. He said 'good night' to *me* ! And smiled !). I didnt see the Duke of Windsor but had a glorious night and a swell dinner and a big fat cigar !

When it was all over, just around 11 o'clock, I walked out of the Connaught Rooms into Kingsway and I was just opposite the Stoll theatre when a very shabby man stopped me and asked if I'd buy a box of matches. I said no thank you, very politely and walked on. He moved quickly and was beside me again asking if I would buy three nice post cards. So I said to him 'Are you really and truly broke – or is this a racket ?'

He said that he was broke and needed 6d. more and then he could get a bed in a place in Waterloo Road.

I have no time for the won't works and the out and out beggers. This man looked down – and I did not want him to be out all night for a tanner. As I was thinking this, he said 'Nice postcards mate' and he winked. So I gave him 6d. for a very grubby envelope which was sealed down. He said 'Thankyou' and moved across the road.

Now, diary, when a man says to a man '*Nice* post

cards' with a wink, 99% times he means *saucy* post cards and they can either be Art Studies and Nudes or they can be those saucy jokes one gets at the sea side. I had got right down to the Strand when I thought to myself, 'Heck, I've paid a tanner, I might just as well look.' So outside the Lyceum Dance Hall I opened that envelope and in there were three picture postcards. Each one was dated 1912. Number one was A View of Blackfriars Bridge. Number two was A View of the Mansion House. Number three was the Duke of Windsor looking about sixteen years of age ! So I saw the Duke of Windsor *after all* !

I stood and laughed ! A policeman standing just a yard from me said 'What's funny ?' So I told him all about it exactly as I've told it to you and he laughed as well. And that's the first time I have seen a policeman laugh for at least five years !

1952

With my own eyes I saw this in print in a USA paper

'Don Hartmann gave a party the other night and pulled a really constructive gag ! He had every guest in the place vaccinated against small pox !'

1952

For the past three weeks on the radio in that popular programme called 'Dear Sir' they have been discussin my very original suggestion that in each town besides a Chamber of Commerce, there should also be a Chamber of Talent where unknown artists in all the branches of Arts and Crafts could go for a little advice (rather like they go to a Poorman's Lawyer).

Everyone is for it. Great idea. Ninety-seven people have written to tell me that they think it's a *very* good idea. What the heck did they think I suggested it for ? Because it was a lousy idea ? Some people – some people just haven't got anything else to do, save waste other peoples time ! But the point of this entry, diary, is that I bet ten to one *nothing* comes of it, like a good many other great ideas ! Still, perhaps I've started a ball rolling. I would like to see A Southwark 'Chamber of Talent' before I die. I feel so lonely. A couple of *local* author-friends would be my delight. There is not a single local author to keep me company ! And the local newspapers are cruel to me.

1952

When will people realise that often in a dirty little puddle in the gutter you can see the reflection of the glorious skies !

1952

I learn from the one and only Boswell that Johnson said to him – I quote – 'He recommended me to keep a journal of my life, full and unreserved. He said it would be a very good exercise, and would yield me great satisfaction when the particulars were faded from my remembrance. I was uncommonly fortunate having had a previous coincidence of opinion with him upon this subject, for I had kept such a journal for some time . . . From this habit I have been enabled to give the world so many anecdotes which would otherwise have been lost to posterity.'

Johnson himself made many many attempts at journal keeping, and for the most part failed at least a dozen times to keep his resolution to keep a regular diary; but Johnson knew the value of diaries, and frequently advised his close friends to keep journals or diaries.

As far as Boswell is concerned, his greatest forte was his zest for life and the fact that he was never self centered. Of course he was an egotist – how on earth can a diarist be anything else ? – but he was always very interested in other people for their own sake. He was at all times interested in things and places, again for the sake of these things rather than for his writings of them.

I would like to always write with the candour of a Pepys or Boswell, but to follow in their paths would be most impudent besides very careless, for I would find myself in most hot water that even dear Stanley Rubinstein would not be able to rescue me from. I will never try to write for any public, putting into my diaries only that which appeals to me and just *hoping* that someday that what Ive written will be pleasant reading for someone else.

A diary writer has to possess a power of detachment, be the actor and the spectator the writer and the reader all in one. Its not easy, but bai jove its a very pleasant occupation.

1952

There was once an author named George Meredith. He was a really celebrated English author and I doubt if anyone would really challenge the statement that he was a master of his craft. I cannot say with hand on heart that I greatly enjoyed 3 novels of his I managed to read from end to end – but they didnt send me to sleep and I did eventually sell them at a fair profit. But in offering my wares I came upon a booklover who was a former Mayor of Camberwell and a reasonably educated man. When I offered the 3 novels by Meredith to him he said he wouldn't have the SWINE in the house !

Now judging by his age I was pretty sure that he had never met up with George and I naturally wondered what the story was behind the really genuine disgust and anger that his words had conveyed to me. It took awhile a quiet conversation in my most expert interviewing manner (and when I set out to interview anyone I *do* get what I want) and then – then I got this. George Meredith it seemed got married and his wife had a child. After awhile husband George and his wife had many quarrels and wife left him.

(Reckon he was *not* an easy man to get along with.) Later, wife returned just to see her child. Meredith refused to allow her to see her child. She haunted the home. She begged on her knees to see her child. Meredith refused all her pleas. Her mind gave out. She became a lunatic and she died in a madhouse solely because of G. Meredith's cruel and callous treatment.

Thats why a former Mayor of Camberwell would not have a G. Meredith work in his Library ! What the hell has how a man treats his wife to do with the book he writes ? Could anything be more darft ? I didnt say this to the silly so and so. After all, I have to sell to live. But I wish I had the brains to write ½ as well as George.

September 1952

A shining light and a kindly light has gone out with the death of Gertrude Lawrence. She was a lady of impulse. Could change in ever varying moods and yet *still* retain the admiration respect and her friends. She was a generous woman and one of the very few stars who was seldom 'catty'. She was in every way a real actress and gave herself whole heartedly to her proffesion right from schooldays. She was to my humble eye born to be an actress, realised that and set out to become a star and a great star she became. Two men will miss her so greatly Mr Aldrich and Mr Coward.

It is over 20 years when I first met her. I had to write about gallerites at the time when they were making such unpleasant scenes at first nights with their boos. Many stars were afraid to comment one way or another for fear that when they read my article they would have it in for the stars if they said anything at all unpleasant. Well, of course, I realised it would be a job but it ment 2 gns to me if I could get the article done and rather bravely I tackled Miss Lawrence on this matter of the patrons of the gallery.

She received me so kindly and I recall how lovely she smelt and what a glorious shining light there was in her eyes. There were several people in her place and they were obviously extremely rich and important people. I was poorly clad and very nervous. I felt so very out of place but she soon put me at ease. I put the question fairly and in a span of 6 seconds I got a reply. 'If we on the stage accept the cheers from the gallery with gratitude we must accept their boos respectfully – and with fortitude.' That was enough. It was just what I wanted. I thanked her. But she would not let me go out into the bitter cold without something hot inside me. I was given a most generous wiskey. I also got a lovely autographed photo. She didn't know me from Adam. I was a stranger. She had no reason to be kind, but she was kind and considerate. From then on I never missed one of her London appearances.

Someday I'll find you! Moonlight behind you. Moonlight or sunshine it will be a long time before there comes a rival to Gertrude Lawrence. I will wear a black tie for the next 3 or 4 days. She was a STAR!

23rd September 1953

Today I visited Chingford and gave what I hope was an amusing informal talk to 400 or so old age pensioners at a Darby and Joan Club at St Emmanuels Hall North Chingford. I must admit frankly that they didn't laugh very often but on the other hand I never saw anyone go to sleep. It was a hard job to hold them as it was a large hall with no loud speaker and 50% of them nearly deaf!

On the train coming back from Chingford to Liverpool Street I learnt to my delight and amazement that the guards name was Ted Bason. I had to have a chat with him in the ernest hope he was some relation. But, alas, it turns out he came from Dorset and so did his father and I've never seen Dorset. He was he said delighted to meet me. He's 57, 5ft 6 fat tubby and jolly. He's like I'd *like* to be at 57 – but in features he is not the slightest bit like me.

I showed him books I'd written. He said he was no hand at reading. I offered to give him a free copy but he said it was my living and he wouldn't expect me to have a free train journey just because a Bason was in the guards van ! All in all a really happy meeting. I'd never never have known of this Bason but for the thoughtfullness of Mrs Quick who by chance heard that on that route of rail there was a Bason and quickly went out of her way to bring us together. There are such a lot of nice people in this world and my fans are amongst them. I wonder if anyone would have written to tell Somerset Maugham that there was a guard named Maugham if he would have gone out of his way to await a certain train and so meet Maugham ? Maybe he would. I just dont know. But I can record the genuine delight I had in meeting Ted Bason – even though he's 'no hand at reading'.

30th December 1953

As we draw towards the close of this year there are 2 items I must put into my Diary which seem to have no headings but mustn't be left out. Both are pleasant. If I was to be asked who are my favourite actors I would say with no hesitation Alec Clunes Marius Goring and Noël Coward. Well, now, diary, Alec Clunes sent 2 nice circle seats to me so that I could take Lizzie to see him in *Carrington V.C.* at the Westminster Theatre. Then out of the blue (and I mean just that) Marius Goring sent a stall seat for me to see *Anthony and Cleopatra* in which he was the star. Its really astounding when you come to think of it. In 2 days 2 stars send tickets and I would bet that neither knew the other was sending (thats if Alec has ever met Marius). Its what can be called a million to one odds. And what did Mr Noël Coward do ? Mr Coward don't *have* to do anything except keep alive.

The second (or third) unexpected joy is an invitation to

attend the Chelsea Arts Ball as a guest of the management! James Agate once said to me: 'When you make the grade, Fred, your trouble will not be where to go but where *not* to go. You will be given free seats and invitations here and there. Look for the catch. There is usually a catch in free gifts and they are not really free.'

Well, dear James, I'm getting up in the grade. But I am sure that in the seats to shows for Marius and Alec and The Arts Ball invite from Loris Rey there is no catch at all. Therefore I feel I must include these happy items at the close of an eventfull happy (on the whole) year.

13th January 1954

Today I had a letter from Doultons, famous china factory on the Albert Embankment asking if I could supply *The ABC to Continental Pottery*, which Unwin published many years ago – and which so badly needs reissuing – I have never seen a copy. Now, although I had a severe cold and was downright poorly and to cap it all it was pouring cats and dogs I went out ½ mile to phone box and phoned the 4 best possible scources in London to try to get this book for them although I knew even if I obtained it there would be no profit in it for me as the price would be top heavy and allow no margin as this is a book which so seldom comes into the market. I failed to locate a copy. I had to write to them my regrets and give them names of Heffer in Cambridge and Blackwell at Oxford who just by chance might have this book because its a guide book which they would have in stock if they could get it and I *have* seen books on china and pottery in both these splendid shops. Why did I trouble? I know no one at all at Doultons! It so happens that just before the war I purchased a Doulton figure of a lovely young lady (have an idea she was called SPRING). She was very refreshing and although in my study she often got dusty, with carefull washing she always came up fresh and springlike again. I ought to have removed her from my mantle piece in the Blitz but I thought – to heck, she can keep me company till either of us die ! One morning after a very heavy raid, I found her on the floor dead – broken in 3 pieces – although Bill Shakespeare in bronze still stood on the shelf gazing down at her. I tried to stick Spring together but somehow she didn't look so nice or refreshing patched up so I put her in the dustbin with my sincere regrets. She was the only piece of Doulton ware I ever owned, and I got her from a high class jumble sale in, of all places, Park Lane. I was sorry not to be able to oblige Doultons. Their craftsmen have given the world much pleasure.

Friendship Ring. March 1954

Useless but touching information.

I've been told today about the Giraffe Women of Burma. Well, they are odd, but most of us know about them or have seen them at exhibitions here and there. But here's the thing I didn't know – at the back of the coils of wire around their necks is a ring that's curled into the coil and this is called a Friendship Ring. When in childhood or youth a boy and girl form a friendly attachment, the man gives the girl a ring which is put at the back of her coil. She may never marry the friend, but can at any time for the rest of her life, call on him for advice or money aid or to fight her battles. Well, it's a nice thought, but what does she give him ? A stiff neck ?

1954

And here's a good one from Frank Swinnerton's novel *Young Felix* :

'In life there are neither rewards nor punishments. There are consequences.'

I wish I'd thought of that one. Thats the sort of work they put at the bottom of day calendars with thoughtfull quotations each day. I've yet to see Mr Swinnerton's one on my calendar. Its too good to miss so I diary it.

A Meeting with Chaliapine (*written 1954*)

Each time that I pass the Adelphi Theatre I recall the night that it was reopened after being entirely rebuilt. It was, I remember, a nasty foggy night and I happened to be in Seven Dials off the Charing Cross Road – and there of all places I found Chaliapine. There were a couple of harpies by him and a very old man, and to these people he was saying one word ADELPHI ! ADELPHI !

Now you couldn't mistake the impressive figure of this great Russian bass. He had a majestic personality even on a foggy night. His audience just stared at him, but I said,

'You – want – The Adelphi *Theatre* ? Opening-to-night-Adelphi-Theatre ?' (You know how you speak to foreigners as if they are foreigners, little children or just darft.) I said the words out loud and slowly. He nodded.

'I can take you. Follow me. You will be quite safe with me !' (He was quite 6 ft 4 and 16 stone. I was 5 ft 4 and 8 stones. He could have picked me up with either hand and thrown me yards.)

We must have looked a very odd pair – a real Mutt and Jeff or The Long and The Short of it – as the fog swallowed us up, but in the Kingdom of the Blind its the man with one eye who is King and for 12 minutes I was the King. It took me 12 minutes to lead him through back alleys down the side of Covent Garden and to the Strand. We did not talk at all. It was far too foggy and unpleasant for casual conversation and indeed I didn't know *what* to talk about.

It was about 10.15 when we got to The Adelphi and as we reached it and I said 'Here you are – all safe and sound !' he shook my hand and crushed my fingers. In the anguish of the moment I had a brain wave and said '*Souvenier* ! Photo *signed* ! Souvenier !' And I gave him a small envelope with my address on it (and a stamp on it as well). He nodded as if he understood my request. We parted. Three days later he sent me a 10 x 8 photograph signed 'Souvenier ! Chaliapine' and enclosed in this envelope my own small envelope. He also sent a handsome gramophone record of himself singing The Flea. Its always been the greatest mystery to me why this rich man hadn't found a taxi that foggy night; how he came to be landed in Seven Dials when he wanted the Strand – and if he really understood English because he said only *one* word during the whole of that meeting, 'ADELPHI'.

April 1954

It is to be noted that Sir Gladwyn Jebb, by virtue of outstanding abilities and astounding devotion to his career has now become our Ambasador in Paris. He is whats called our Plenipotentiary to France, although what the heck that is exactly I've no idea. Its a jolly important position and carries with it a huge salary and even huger expenses allowances which I am sure this bloke will earn with dignity. He's ever so dignified. Why do I put him in my diary ? Well, he's about the most English Englishman I've ever come upon. Always well groomed. Never at a loss for words. Never seems to be out of salts. A product of the old school tie – ETON and Oxford I think. Mark you, I've never spoken to him – I wouldn't have the cheek, but of all Englishmen I've ever come upon he is my idea of an English *Gentleman*.

Duff Cooper, who was our Ambassador before Jebb, was a literary man and I did have 2 conversations with him – on Viscount Grey and his writings. I wonder what Sir Gladwyn reads outside *The Times* ? It would be interesting to find out.

Heard on the Radio, 1953

'My most precious possession is a hot water bottle that was once owned by Cleopatra – hardly been used.'

August 1954

This month I stayed 2 days in a vicarage for the first time in my life. Indeed, first time I'd ever *entered* a vicarage or had a vicar as my host. Blimey they didn't once say 'Grace' at any meal at all. I wonder wether they stopped because I was there – or wether they dont know Grace – or wether its a dying out fashion. Me, I think its a nice fashion and I always says Grace – not aloud but to myself. I have been hungry in my time. I know what an empty belly feels like – so I am grateful for a meal. *All* people ought to be !

29th August 1954

As one grows older, birthdays usually pass unnoticed, but today, my birthday has been exceptionally interesting. Anton Dolin allowed me to attend a full rehearsal of a new ballet called 'Napoli'. During it a beautiful ballet star, Daphne Dale, spent a great deal of her spare time reading a book. I felt bound to enquire as to the title of same and was rather astounded when Anton found out for me that she was reading, with apparent keenness and enjoyment, *Anna of the Five Towns* by Arnold Bennett. How the author would have enjoyed knowing this and meeting Miss Dale. She is a real smasher – and so very talented as well. Mrs Frank Pettingell gave me a lovely pullover for a birthday gift. Mrs Morris in Birmingham sent me a Max Murrey thriller, and my dear Lizzie gave me an electric razor. I also had eight cards. All in all a very wonderful birthday.

W.H.Berry. 1955

Last year whilest in the company of Anton Dolin at The Festival Hall I was introduced to Ethel Levey. I think Anton thought I was slipping a little that I didnt bring out my album and capture the autograph of this one time musical comedy star. But how was he to know that I got her autograph in 1927 when she was appearing in a show called The Blue Kitten at The Gaiety Theatre in London. And how could I tell Ethel, who was certainly no chicken but was dressed to kill in a style that would possibly have suited a woman 30 years younger, that I saw her 30 years ago ! Most ladies dislike being reminded of past glories with the possible exceptions of Sybil Thorndike, Edith Evans and Flora Robson, who don't seem to mind – or at least are too clever or too ladylike to show *your* lack of tact. But Ethel Levey was one who would mind. However, as we left together in the lift from Anton's dressing room, I was able to say that I hoped she would taxi round and see The Gaiety Theatre as I heard it was soon to be pulled down. I had tact not to say as an old has-been.

I remember The Blue Kitten for one very good reason : it was the first show I obtained the signatures of everyone in the cast. It took several weeks to accomplish this pleasant task. Some of the lesser known chorus ladies were extremely reluctant to sign – till I plodded them with 'I suppose you *are* able to write your own name – besides being *beautifull* !' That usually worked. And the chorus men must have thought there was a catch in it. They were positively refusing for all manner of reasons, till I showed them all the *stars* autographs and then said, 'Blimey, if they can, why not you ? Are you all that important ? I only want to complete a most pleasant task – the complete cast – *even you.*' That 'even you' got them ! I can still find 57 'Blue Kitten' autographs but, alas, most of them are today quite forgotten people.

There's one in that group I will never quite forget and thats W. H. Berry. I dont know if hes alive today (I hope so) but I remember him as a cheerfull, kindly, amiable man who off stage really did *look* a comic. He had a merry red face and was a fat and jolly man. He weighed all of 16 stone when I was bearly 6 stone. If I stood behind him I was completely hidden. I really believe two of me could have stood behind him and not been seen. He was a wide man, with a delightful sense of humour. When I asked him for his autograph he said 'Where shall I put it, sonny ?' Of course he ment on which page as I held out a large album. Quick as a flash I said,

'Oh you'd *better put it on a cheque* !'

He stared at me.

'*What* did you say, sonny ?'

I said, 'You'd better put it on a cheque. That will suit *me* proper alright, mister.'

Straight away he gave me back my album and from his inside coat pocket he got out a cheque book. Then he put the book up against the wall beside the Gaiety stage door and asked me my full name – which I told him – Frederick Thomas Bason. He wrote it out in full. Then he looked at me and then back again at the cheque and said 'How much shall I fill it in for ?'

'Oh, I leave that to *you*,' I said. I didn't *dare* name a figure although I knew his salary exceeded one hundred pounds a week and that he was always in work. Well, he filled in a figure – it was for TUPPENCE. He didn't put Twopence. He wrote 'Tuppence', after he'd crossed out the pounds sign and he signed it with a flourish.

'Here you are, my boy. The customer *has* to be pleased !' he said handing me the cheque.

And I really and truly was pleased. If it had been for over 2s. I might have been tempted to cash it, when things were tough for me, but as it was I keepted that 2d. cheque for years and years.

There is a rather nice ending to this recollection. There I stood at the stage door with cheque in one hand and album in the other. Berry walked through the door and then suddenly turned round and came back to my side.

'I rather think you had an idea I was going to make it a large sum of money.'

'Oh no, sir, really I didnt. I only said it as a lark. After all, you did leave yourself wide open when you asked where should you put your autograph !'

'Yes I suppose I did. Well, for your cheek or your politeness here's 10s. Yes, take it – to please me. You've given me a nice little tale to tell at the Club and a good tale is *always* worth paying for.'

He then raised his hat to me and went back through the stage door. I never met him close to again – ever. He was a really nice man and a born comedian.

After reading the Third Diary – a reader's letter.
14th January 1956

You are, of course, what is known as a Neo Primitive and for that reason I write my appreciation of your book. It is a very rare thing to be and occurs sometimes among painters. The most famous was Le Douanier Rousseau in Paris in the late 19th Century. Grandma Moses in U S A is another and Madame Delacroix in the South of France is another. There is supposed to be a fisherman painter in Cornwall (name like Tenby, Henby) but I don't think he is really good enough for the title. Certainly I didn't know one existed in this country until I read your book though I have heard many claims.

A neo primitive is an unusual mixture. One minute one thinks they are naive and innocent – the next minute they seem to know more than the sophisticates. They follow a razor edge between the child and the wise old man without ever falling into Middle Age.

The strangest thing about them is that they never imitate the professional painter or writer. Most people, when they begin to grasp technique, start to try and be professional. The Neo Primitive never does though I cannot think what stops them. Its a very good job they don't but I don't know why they don't.

Many professional painters would like to paint in the Neo Primitive way but they can't. I can't – though my children can. But when they get to 14 they no longer can.

So there you are – rare and fortunate – the only worth while Neo Primitive in the country.

You should read of Le douanier Rousseau sometime. He's your spiritual elder brother.

And thank you for a stimulating experience.

Yours,

R. MYERSCOUGH-WALKER

On Diaries (written 1956)

I think that during the past thirty years I have come upon near enough 100 published diaries. I very seldom pass one thats reasonably priced that I have not read. I dont think of the possiable profit I may take on a resale after a reading so much as will it hold my attention or tell me anything about the difficult art. Usually a glance tells me if it will interest me and I dont suppose I have passed over more than twenty against the 100 Ive purchased. Fortunately they all sold later. . .for I just cannot afford to hoard books. I think if I ever get rich enough or famous enough to write to make a slim living and have a little over I will gather together a diary or journal collection as company for my old age but I will be a bit choosy in my selection. I rather think it would be a good idea this afternoon (its ever so wet and I've nothing else to do) to compile a list of around forty diaries that have in some way or another interested me. They may form something of a check list for collectors of this form of art. I cannot put them into any real order of merit, although Pepys Boswell and Bennett are probally my three favourites with the great Ben Haydon a close up 4th. Well, here goes – the result of thirty years attention. The side notes are as I wrote at the time of reading.

William Allingham : *A diary*. He was a man of letters and

met folks like Tennyson. Its a very readable book although of corse a period piece. Nicely written and not dull.

James Beattie : his *London Diary*, He knew Dr Johnson. A very human piece of work. Period around 1775.

A. Bennett : *Four Journals*. A joy for anyone. (3 forming one group, 1 diary another.)

Boswell's *Private Papers*. A work of great art.

Fanny Burney : *Diary and Letters* in six vols. Was edited by A. Dobson. Period pieces but what pieces – and what a nice piece *she* was and all !

Jane Carlyle : *Letters and Memorials* (ed. Froude). I didnt enjoy this work as a *whole*.

Lady Clifford's Diary. V. Sackville West edited it. Very enjoyable.

The Creevey Papers by T. Creevy in two vols. Most interesting. 1810 to around 1820 period, and a very colourfull period at that.

The diary of William Dyott. Period twenty years or so each side of 1800. I *dont* like this. . .found it rather dull reading here and there. Second half the best.

John Evelyn : his *Diary* (ed. Dobson). An absolute JOY. Read it *three* times. I wish Dobson was alive to edit *my* Diary.

Through England on a side saddle in the time of William and Mary by C. Fiennes. A grand journal, and one I shall always remember because it was the first diary I ever made a handsome profit on when I resold it, my client having searched England (*not* on a side saddle) for twenty years to find a copy. Mine was the 1888 edition and in deep brown cloth. 9 by 6 and very clean copy. I got 16s. for it.

Caroline Fox : *The Journal of C. Fox* (ed. W. Harris). Not my cup of tea as a whole. But here and there most interesting.

The Life of Elizabeth Fry compiled from her journals.

Colourfull and brave lady who did a lot of good. I found this interesting from end to end.

The works of Edward Gibbon. It was in five vols., and after vol. one I gave 'em up – but fortunately sold at a small profit. But some would like Gibbon.

The Greville Memoirs by C. Greville. Sent me to sleep. But could be weeded from a huge work into a very nice little book, as here and there okay.

Vine Hall, Bookseller. The autobiography of the author of *The Sinners' Friend*. A very interesting work. Pub. 1874. Well worth attention; enjoyable.

Benjamin Haydon : *Life of B. Haydon* (ed. Taylor). An absolute masterpiece.

The Diary of R. Hooke (ed. Adams and Robinson). Period 1675 (roughly). This is an unusual diary. A 'must' for diary readers.

Samuel Johnson : praise be for Mr Boswell !

Kilvert's *Diary* (ed. Plomer). A very lovely diary. . .a breath of fresh air.

The Diary of a Bankrupt Bookseller. A fake but an absolute joy. This is a darling of a book, and all true booklovers will find it a pleasure.

The *Diaries* of W. C. Macready. Pub. 1912 in two vols. Worth looking at, as here and there quite outstanding.

The Journal of K. Mansfield (ed. by her husband). Enjoyable, and beautifully edited with loving care. This Journal will live when her tales are no more fashionable.

The Diary of Ben Newton : rector of Wath. Difficult to find – worth having ! Worth seeking.

Pepys. Well, just anything in its a delight, especially Wheatleys edition. He is the daddy of them all, and the world owes him a great debt. Pepys is my master – all my life.

The Diary etc. of H. Crabb Robinson. Period 1811 to near

1870. Robinson was a very lively man I would have loved to have met. He was no crab !

The Life, Letters and Journals of Lord John Russell. Another man I would have enjoyed meeting, even though he was a LORD.

The Diaries of John Ruskin. Not much in my line of country but o.k. in parts. Readable in small doses.

A. Ponsonby : *English Diaries. More English Diaries* etc. They are MUSTS for all who ever wish to collect diaries. They are more than check lists, they are really wonderfull labours of love, and Arthur Ponsonby and me would get on well together. Is he alive ? Oh I do hope so.

Scotts Last Expedition. A classic. Will stand the stress of time.

The Journal of Sir Walter Scott. Heres a mighty work, a classic indeed. What a Diary it would have been if recorded for a longer period.

The Life and the Letters of Mary W. Shelley. Period 1815 to about '40. Here is a grand book that will live many a generation. I've never found a diary by her brother. I would have liked to have had tea with Mary. She had an original mind.

The Diary of Henry Slingsby. A masterly diary, one *not* to miss, but is rare.

Ralph Thoresby : *The Diary of R. Thoresby,* two vols. Period roughly 1700. Extremely readable, a *must* for the true diary lover – but *not* the general reader.

The Journal of John Wesley. Of all people Arnold Bennett said this was an excellent bedside book. I have found better ones !

The Journals of Dorothy Wordsworth. Absolutely splendid. *Not* to be missed !

The Diary of a Country Parson by James Woodforde, in five vols. Go the whole of the route, for this is well worth the endurance test.

The Journal of a disappointed Man. W. N. P. Barbellion. A masterpiece – held me spellbound.

The Diary of John Yeoman to London. Pub. 1934 but is of the 1770s, and is a real delight. Here was a lively man. He and Sam Pepys would have got along so well together.

We must not *quite* forget that Queen Victoria had a bash at journal writing; will I be told I'm unpatriotic if I say that *Leaves from the Journal* etc. bored me to blooming tears and we were NOT even amused?

The Polderoy Papers by Vulliamy are fakes but very very clever and worth the reading. One almost wishes they were true.

Then finally we must *not* miss out *Knole and the Sackvilles* by Victoria Sackville West for no library would not be complete without this good book.

Looking Back (*written 1956*)

I read my first book by L. A. G. Strong way back in 1932, and came upon it in a rather strange manner. I was going to the Crystal Palace in May of that year to see a white hope of heavyweight boxing named Jack Doyle. (He wasn't much of white hope – more green than white.) On my way I looked into a bookshop and my eye caught a title by Strong called *Doyle's Rock*. It struck me as a rather nice coinsidence that I was actually on my way to see Doyle and that his opponant would very probaly make him ROCK, that I purchased this book for 2s. 6d. It was under my arm as I watched Jack Doyle win by a knockout his fight in the first round with one hefty haymaker that the oponent saw coming but forgot to duck.

I immediately went to the dressing room to try to get the autograph of this White hope, but from excitement or perhaps in those days he was not able to write (well I have known heavyweights who were quite unable either to read or to write, and yet they made several thousands with their fists before they retired and opened pubs), I was not able to get his autograph at this start to his career. He said, 'Another time.'

It was all of 15 years later, at the very close of his career when he was and would have admitted he was an has been, when he was a small turn at The New Cross Empire variety house where he was trying to sing and failing noblely to amuse that he, in a very humble and most kindly manner obliged me with his autograph.

Doyle was a winner that day, and I found *Doyles Rock* to be a winner as well. It is a group of 14 short stories, and everyone of the fourteen extreemly readable. Now, I've never been very fond of short stories – even those of Maugham – but I greatly enjoyed 12 out of the 14 in that book which is a very high average; and I enjoyed them for one very good reason, they got on with the job. There was a start, a middle and each one ended. They were Short Stories.

The term short stories has for some years been stretched to cover a whole term of work which has just nothing whatever to do with the art of story telling : things like prose poems, psychological studies, personality pieces and chilly bits of atmospheric happenings that have no plot no story.

In my youth men like Conrad Galsworthy Arnold Bennett and Maugham told stories. Somerset Maugham in *Summing Up* gave the best bit of advice to would be writers of short stories. I am sure he wont really mind if I repeat it here : 'The short story must have a definite design. . . a design which includes a point of departure,' a climax and a point of rest, in other words its got to have a PLOT. Maugham says that 'the chief use of a plot is that its a line to direct the reader's interest'.

This is possibly the most important thing in fiction. How well he puts it. Of course thats it, and when a story has no 'line' then the readers attention wavers and his interest is LOST!

In 12 of the tables in *Doyle's Rock* my attention never wavered and I considered that I had a very good value for my 2s. 6d. I then sought out some of Strongs novels and in turn read *The Brothers, The Jealous Ghost* and *Dewar Rides,* and enjoyed the three of them. I then set about meeting the author, and wrote an amiable letter enclosing a stamped addressed envelope, and asking for his autograph. I got a kind reply in four days. Two more letters passed between us and then we met, and we have been friends ever since.

Mark you, we do not get into each others hair. If we meet once in ten months its a pretty good average. But we have in common a genuine love of books, and he is one of the very few men I know who can talk books till the cows come home, and the time speeds by.

I think Leonard Strong is the most versitile man in the modern world of literature, as a broadcaster, lecturer, singer, short story writer, novelist. He is also a keen boxing fan, and so we have a great deal in common. I learnt the art of lecturing solely by going to his lectures and listening to not only what he said but *how* he said it.

He edited my second diary, at a smaller fee than he would normally have charged. There have been but two men in my life whom I would have liked to have been my dad one is Samuel Looker, the Richard Jefferies expert, and the other is L. A. G. Strong, can one say more?

Further note. His death in 1958 brought a great gap into my life. I lost a real pal who stood by me when some scum in the civil service were doing their uttermost to ruin me.

1956

In a city called Lima way out in S. America there lays in a glass case the mummified body of a man named Pizarro.

Way back in the year 1532 or thereabout this magnificent beast of a Spaniard aided by some 180 other Spaniards defeated Emperor Atahuallpa, the Ruler of the Aztecs, and caused the fall of a great civilisation. Pizarro who was an unwanted foundling left on a church door, started life as a swineherd – and lived with the swine. He died in the gutter. He was, it is said, stabbed by a jealous rival for power, and as Pizarro died he made a cross with his own blood in that gutter, kissed it and died. Ive never read a book on the life of Pizarro nor seen a film about him. I would think that his life would make an epic for any screen and if I could get Mr Orson Wells to be my film Pizarro and had a million pounds to play with to make this film I am pretty sure I could double my money for such a film if made with care would capture a *world* market. It would be called *The Magnificent Beast*.

About 30 years ago – maybe more, I had a little chat with a really famous pioneer film producer named Carl Lehmann or something like that. He was a cherry old man and very American. I put to him the idea that as seeds found in tombs 1000 years old have been taken from these tombs, planted and grew, so the seed of man rejuvenated by the miracle of radium could perhaps be revived and placed into the womb of woman and *bear a son* – the son of a man whos been dead hundreds of years ! Carl said it was too fantastic even for the cinema and was *not* photographic in its theme ! I had *not* heard of Pizarro then. Indeed to my shame I only heard of Pizarro this week although he died about 1550 ! Oh, I wish I'd heard of this great conquistador all those years back for I am sure I *could* have convinced Carl that whilest my 'seed sensation' (as I called it) may not have been filmable, the life of Pizarro with his really cinamagraphic last scene would clean up a fortune. David Lean, please note.

Isn't it a great shame you think of smashing ideas at *odd* times. Good Luck is when preparation meets opportunity.

Now I don't know a soul who would listen to my 'Magnificent Beast' so I write in my Diary because I've got nothing else to write as I've been ill the past 3 weeks so I am *not* feeling MAGNIFICENT.

1956

Two cats sat in front of a fire in perfect harmony. A young man said to an old lady 'Look ! That's what marriage should be. Two people sitting together in perfect harmony.' And the lady said 'Yes, they's all right like that – but you *tie* them together and then there'd be pandemolion !'

Jack Smith. 1956

When I hear the girls rave about Ronnie Hilton, Michael Holliday and Perry Como my mind goes back to the late 1920's when the girls raved about a very ordinary nice man with a very ordinary name. He was Jack Smith. Only for the most part it was debutantes and rich men's daughters and even minor Princesses who raved about Jack Smith. I would say that he had a fan mail that exceeded any male film stars of the period and he still remained an *extraordinary* ordinary nice man. And I will hasten to add that he was an out and out American citizen.

They say that Johnnie Ray can 'make' a song ! Well, so could Jack Smith. But Ray has to sort of beat himself into a frenzy and have bouts of crying and get all worked up and be whats called dynamic to get it over. Mr Smith was ever so cool, extremely calm and never raised his voice above a *whisper* ! Yet you heard every word he whispered and he was enchanting. Even men raved about Jack Smith, 'The Whispering Baritone'. He died at the fairly early age of 51 and was at his death almost a forgotten man – but I believe the day will come when his gramophone records will be collector's pieces (so will those of Gene Austin – another forgotten star of the late 1920's).

Still, diary, I was remembering Jack Smith. He began in show business as a song plugger for Irving Berlin. He frankly admitted to me one evening that he considered himself to be 'a rather poor pianist'. He admitted he *couldn't* sing. And yet he was earning at that time about seven hundred pounds per week (and thats when 700 pounds was *real* money !). He used to charge 100 gns to sing 3 or 4 songs at private parties for 15 minutes *only* – and at the 15th minute he was up from the piano and making for the exit ! And he was booked for months ahead ! But sometimes at night clubs when in the mood he would sing 30 songs, encore after encore and enjoy himself the *whole* time ! He said that he knew 90 songs that he could sing at the drop of a hat.

Fame never never changed Jack and he was an ever welcome visitor to London. I would say that his greatest song hit was 'Blue Skies'. And when he sung it you felt *bound* to join in. I remember him so well not for the getting of his autograph (he was always willing to give that – and unasked add from his jacket pocket a nice photograph) but because once I heard him do a tricky sort of vamp in his piano playing, a jazz off beat rythm which caught my fancy. I had it nearly – but not quite. So I went to the stage door and asked to see him. I saw him and I hummed that tricky bit of jazz playing to him. Please could he teach it to me ? Bless his kind heart. He had never seen me before. I was a rather grubby and shabby chap in my teens and I hadnt £5 in all the world. I was *nothing* to him but he took me back stage and waited 5 or 6 minutes till the interval was on. He then opened the piano and played that vamp 4 times. Then I had to play it. I hadn't quite got it, so he did the last bit again and then I had it. And I had to play it twice before Mr Smith was satisfied that I really had it fixed in my mind. And this took all of 10 minutes. It never occured to me then but probally 500 people were waiting for him at some night club whilest he taught me a tricky catchy little vamp – which I've never ever forgotten ! And dont forget I was a *stranger* to him ! Thats how kind he was.

Yes, the Whispering Baritone was a truly great American star – and such a nice man. In my heart I believe it was his kindness which taught me one thing in life : If you want something from a celebrity ask politely – *but ask*. The greater they are, the nicer they are. And its so strange to record that if I hadn't asked Jack Smith a night club star of 1927 how to vamp I would not have asked Noel Coward in 1956 if I could be his guest and attend once in my life a night club. Strange how things do link up. I wonder if Mr Coward remembers Jack Smith ? I must ask him ! Somehow I have an idea that he will recall the name. There will never be another Jack Smith ! They dont whisper now. They SHOUT !

August 1956

Most times before I give a talk, I say to myself these immortal words from a man named Zimmerman.

'Open your mouth and purse cautiously, and your stock of wealth and reputation shall, at least in repute, be great.'

I pass these few words on to other lecturers and talkers, great and small. This Zimmerman has got something – and when you know a good thing, you should tell it to other people !

October 1956

I called on a woman about some T.S. Eliot books and her husband sat in the same room doing his football pools ! Save for 'Hello' he said nothing to me. He was ever so busy and slung round his neck on a piece of wide blue ribbon was a full-size *horse-shoe* ! I do hope it helped him.

On Baron Corvo. 1956

That grand old man of letters Arthur Machen assured me he had *never* made 100 pounds in any one year from his pen in the whole of his literary career ! And he really was a capital and famous author.

J.D. Beresford was also a very notable author (I dont know if he's still alive) and public librarians always bought his books for they were 'reliable, clean, well constructed novels'. I was assured by a close friend of his that J.D. never exceeded 200 pounds a year from his pen. I am myself in the J.D. cart. I usually exceed Arthur's annual but *never* J.D.'s.

Now we come to F. Rolfe, the self styled Baron Corvo. The demand for his books far far exceeds the supply. For every copy I get (irrespective of the condition) I can find 30 buyers – for my one copy. Now this is the point. Rolfe didn't make ONE hundred pounds from his literary works during the *whole* of his unfortunate life ! Yet today put together any 3 of his first editions in fine clean sound condition and you have one hundred pounds ! The irony of it all. Baron Corvo many many time starved and was utterly broke. Mark you, for the most part it was his own silly fault. He sponged on his few friends and was one of the worlds most insolent men plus a huge unnessersary liar – but lets give a little credit : he *did* write some extremely remarkable books. Each year they get more and more popular and each year they get *scarcer*. There will come a day when (and I'm not talking through my hat) an immaculate first edition of one of his earliest books will realise one hundred pounds in an auction room. Yes, Diary, I'm positive by the law of supply and demand that one of his books will make £100 – more money than Rolfe made in *all* his life ! They ought to make a film of his awfull tragic life. Symon's *Quest for Corvo* excites anyone to read Corvo. You cant be sorry for the man – but if you have a love of the unusual in literature, then you cannot help but admire many of his books. He had a very ornamental colourfull pen – but I wish to God I could paint half as well !

20th May, 1957

A staggering piece of information told me by a boy of 12 today. I asked him what he wanted to be when he was older and he said a minister. I asked him what he was doing now and he said he was learning to be an *actor*. I then said 'Well, surely that wont help you to become a *Minister*,' and with all the calmness in the world he said, 'Maybe it will. I have been told that ministers who fail to make the grade often become actors – so I'm learning both !' And he is twelve ! Aint modern youth staggering ?

August 1957

'Oh yes, I saw the war. France, Germany, Burma, Singapore – I saw it *all*. Yes, I've done my bit !'

Yes, he was the projectionist at the Coronet Cinema – the so and so !

Exact conversation reheard by a pal of mine in the pub in Lambeth, and retold on a post card to me as funny. Is it funny ? Strange as it may seem, it didn't even make me smile.

1957

I feel so very sad today. Frank Tilsley, the novelist, has killed himself. There is no doubt at all about that. Of all the men I know he was the *last* one I would have thought would ever do that ! So practical so sensible, so down to earth. I remember our first meeting. It was on September 29th, 1950. On television there was a series called 'Designed for Women' and by some wonderfull manner (probally my pal Norman Collins pulling a string) Frank Tilsley was reviewing my First Diary in this actual programme and I was asked to go along to face some questions on the art of being a diarist.

After Frank had said my work was strangely moving and startling truthfull and so very readable, I was asked to speak about myself. It was not a question and answer. Mr Tilsley gave me the floor and a full couple of minutes and I really let myself go. I gave myself some pretty good plugs and Frank just smiled as if at a clever son doing his party piece and he never shut me up once ! And it was *his* show ! It was *his* Book corner. I was just no one. He had me there and could have told me to put a sock in it or taken the words out of my mouth and left me high and dry but he just smiled on me – and on I went, having the time of my life.

I couldn't imagine J. B. Priestley or Alan Dent allowing me any scope to shine in. Frank being a down to earth working class author understood that it was my one moment of glory, my one chance to plug my writings – and he let me get on with it. Only Wilfrid Pickles would have done that besides Frank. Those 2 minutes he gave me caused Diary One to sell 10,000 copies. I am sad. Ive lost a pal – and my sympathy goes out to his family. I've never met his family but most of his many letters to me contained mention of them and I felt I knew all of them. I've also lost an editor. I longed for Frank Tilsley to edit Diary 5. He'd have made such a lovely editor.

Oh, I best place on record the fact that Leonard Merrick gave me the idea that any diaries of mine should each have a different editor, as each of his books had a different introducer.

October 1957

The late but ever great G. K. Chesterton once found himself on a long dull railway journey with nothing whatever to read, so on odd pieces of paper he wrote an essay as he explored the contents of his pockets. If you ever come upon a group of his essays containing 'What I found in my pockets' buy the book for this gem of an essay. I don't think anyone could have written better.

I am now on a dreary journey to the North to give a lecture and Ive finished the novel I've brought with me (*Slaves of Solitude* by Patrick Hamilton) and I'm going to try to write an essay called 'It will be safe in there'. I wouldn't have the impudence to ape G.K.C. by looking into my own pockets – although one day I *will* explore my wallet.

Warwick Deeping 20 years ago said in giving advice 'See that the carbon is in the right way, then put the title on the work in capital letters and add the date you started the work, and then get *on* with it.' I've done title and date. I'm using a pen on a pad of writing paper in a rather unsteady train.

Start your essay with a Bang ! Well, how about this ? Hundreds of people must have put things inside the pages of books as they said to themselves 'It will be safe inside there –' and then *forgot* the book they put it in ! Hence you come upon odd things inside old books. I remember so well the time I bought a book from a stall in East Street, Walworth, and found in the last page of the text (before the end paper) when I could get it apart a remarkably filthy dirty indecent real photograph of a man and woman and I knew of *both* of them ! One was a former Mayor of C——— and a well-known personality. The woman was a cashier in a local cinema. I knew both by sight and the photo (a flash light one) was so clear. It could have ruined either of them. I immediately tore it into small pieces and burnt them (word of honour). What madness ! Anyone could have bought that novel (by Haggard) for sixpence ! A nasty man or woman would have blackmailed either. It was an astoundingly indecent picture and if you saw that woman in any street you'd think she was a Sunday School teacher ! I saw that man several times after I destroyed that picture – but somehow in a *new* light. The woman went to greater heights. She got a man but *not* the one in the photo. She is a very handsome woman. Last time I saw her it was at a film premire with an American officer.

The only bit of luck I ever found in a book was 12s. 6d. in saving stamps in the front endpaper of another novel. Again I had to pull the pages apart as the gum from the back of the stamps had caused the endpaper to stick down fast. I cashed them.

I never again found money. Strangest thing I found was a dozen Hongkong tram tickets used as book markers in a dictionary and strange as it may seem I found a man who really collected bus and train tickets and he was delighted to buy them ! I got *more* for the dozen tickets than I got for the dictionary. I did actually see a fellow bookseller find a £5 note in a hymn book. I missed it because looking along the row of books I didn't even touch the hymn book. But he looked inside it (he said he thought it might contain a Victorian silk book marker) and when he found the fiver he was delighted to give 6d. for the book !

Oh, I forgot. I did find a small block of Edward the 7th stamps in a B. M. Croker novel – but only ½d. stamps. And now I recall them to mind I remember they were stuck down to the actual title page of the novel. 12 half-penny stamps – probally been there donkies years !

Its a rule of booksellers to always destroy letters they may find in books no matter what sort of letters. I only once neglected to do this when I found a rather charming letter from Jerome K. Jerome who wrote 3 *Men in a Boat*. It was only wishing someone well and seemed a pity to be destroyed.

Its never safe to put things into books. They are *never* really safe there. You are liable to forget the book – or die before you can put the thing somewhere else ! Or some-one has a loan of the book. But I've done it myself. I had a rather nice photograph of film star Joan Bennett. It got rather crushed in the post so temporarly I put it in a book to flatten it out. A librarian called when in a buying mood and he bought 100 novels. I never found my photo of Joan again. It went to the Library and I couldn't say the title of the novel for I'd forgotten. I only remembered too late that I'd temporary put it in one of the books in a pile on the floor and when you have 10,000 vols thats *most* unwise !

Of course, there are fake books, that are really boxes. One always gets a genuine thrill when such a 'book box' comes one's way. You just *never* know what you will find on opening it up. Most of them are empty but I did come upon one in a tied up pile of books and that contained a set of false teeth, a lock of hair, 3 short Victorian hat pins, a tiny carved statue of some sort of saint and a postcard picture of a man in China having his head cut off by a soldier – card dated 1906. What an odd lot.

During war time, when books changed hands so quickly one often found ration cards in books and wondered if the former owners of them were dead. I would point out ration cards not only of the past war but of the 1914-1918 one as well ! Once when I had my bookshop a lady came back after selling me a large bundle of books, begging permission to go through them. I gave her permission. She took a copy of *Westward Ho* by Kingsley and there flattened and cutting into pages before and after it was a tiny narrow gold ring – hers. I hadn't looked into the book. I'd merely glanced at the titles, asked her price and paid it. She said it had been her ring as a child. You could hardly believe that a ring of all things could be put into a book and not *fall out* but this one had cut so deep into the text that when the book was shut up you'd never never think a gold ring was inside it. I hadn't the heart to tell her that *Westward Ho* was destroyed for me as the round rings of that little ring had gone through a ¼ of the book. She was overjoyed at finding it. I bet she found a safer place in the future !

I've found old Lottery tickets being used as book markers and wondered what on earth would have happened if one of those tickets had WON – and the owner had passed the book on with the ticket in it. He'd never have had a hope of recovering it, and the new owners might never have realised its value. (This seems like a plot for a novel or a film called The Lottery Ticket.) A bookseller pal found in a book a ticket – only a gallery seat – for the Pallidium and he went and saw Tommy Trinder in a show there. He bought the book on a bookstall on a Saturday. The ticket was for the following Tuesday. He said he'd have been willing to have paid had the real owner recalled the number of his or her seat – but no one showed up. That was frightfully careless – or a small chapter of accidents. Time again I've found phone numbers jotted down on odd scraps of paper and put in books for safety – but Ive never had the curiosity to ring up one of the numbers.

We who sell books HATE silver paper or flowers or grass to be placed in books. These things brown the pages and soil the books. Press a flower in a book and you'll find a year later a horrible stain that *nothing* gets out ! I saw a lovely *Alice in Wonderland* quite ruined with dozens of rose petals pressed into it. A £200 copy was soiled to the extent that it sold for £25 as every page of the text was soiled by the stains from the petals. Sentimental may be, but silly as well.

We are now nearing Manchester and the man opposite me says we shall be there in 4 or 5 minutes. I started these memories when we were at Bedford (I think) and its whiled away the time in a nice manner. The man beside me has been looking at this MSS from behind the cover of his paper. Perhaps he thinks its a long love letter (I wish it was). I want to finish it before I get to Manchester or I have a feeling I wont ever end this essay. Perhaps I'll stick it in a book and say 'It will be safe inside there' and then I will sell the book and the original MSS. Well, maybe thats all its worth ? No ! No ! Its worth *more* than that because it has served its purpose. Its killed a dull journey. I wonder if G. K. Chesterton had the same satisfaction as I am feeling at the moment – the satisfaction of having set out to complete a small task and completed it.

Oh, Ive just recalled that I found the genuine autograph of Nellie Melba on a slip of paper inside a copy of *The Blue Lagoon*. It was quite authentic as I already had her signature. I bet someone was wild about losing that ! And I remember a librarian telling me years ago he found a plan of an office and a safe combination in a book. But he never found out which office or which safe or where !

I suppose before I put on my overcoat and get down my lecture case I ought to put the obvious moral of these recollections which is that *nothing* is safe inside a book – and never will be in this speedy age. And before anyone sells books to booksellers they really ought to go through every page of every book to see that nothing is put between its pages ! Its ever so silly to put an intimate letter inside the novel you happen to be reading and then forget about it – after saying 'It will be safe in there'. It wont be safe and it will *not* remain intimate and you may well live to regret it – so stop using foolish things as book markers ! And to cap it all another librarian said he visited a slum home and he found a kipper – an oily one – being used as a book marker !

And now we are in Manchester.

1957

The justly celebrated American author Tennessee Williams (*Glass Menagerie* etc.) is reputed to have said these words recently. I quote : 'I dont trust any writers views about his own work. His views are worth nothing. He should please his audience on his own terms.' End of statement.

I suppose Mr Williams knows – after all he's a terrific success and probally a very rich author now. But somehow I just dont agree with him. I says and I've said it these 25 years, you are very often just as good as you think you are and if you think your work smells then by Golly it *does*. An authors views on his own work *are* worth something – they will always be worth something. Sometimes you have to please your public on *their* terms. We can't *all* be Tennessee Williams !

Strange People these Japanese. December 1957

I have it on pretty good authority that the Japanese are omnivorous readers of almost every sort of publication and have very probally the highest literacy rate in the world. There is at least one bookshop in every district of every city or town in Japan. Big cities have collections of shops selling every sort of book – that puts Charing X Rd in the shade. Books rank as a necessity in Japan ! (I wish to God they did in London – here they are an occasional luxury.) Mark you, Japanese people have always spelt Culture with a Big C. Culture really matters out there and authors and philosophers get immense respect. (In London you are looked upon as 'queer' if you are either !)

The turnover from printed matter in Japan each year runs into millions ! And yet they have (I'm told) the most cumbersome difficult and indeed most inefficient language in *all* the world ! This seems extremely strange. If G.B. Shaw had left cash to reform the Japanese language he would have done a *great* deal of good. He would not only have made future generations very happy but he would have done much to have keepted the peace of the East. By books the friendships of the world grow stronger – and they *do* buy books in Japan but with such a difficult language to learn they must find the reading of books an extremely difficult task and a labour of LOVE !

To be omnivorous readers of every kind of book in the worlds most difficult language seems to me very wrong. I cannot do much about it – save comment. But they can have the rights of my first Diary for *nothing* if it will help to bring about a more lasting peace out there and give some Japanese an insight into the ways of The Strange English.

One final point, diary. I've always been strangely attracted to a pretty Japanese girl. The pretty ones are really very pretty – not that I've ever spoken to one yet. I cannot even say Yes or No or I Love You in Japanese – yet !

A sample of Charlie Chester's wit. Said in 1958

Mr Macmillan wants to go to the West Indies, but he can't get a permit from Noël Coward.

January 1958

102 requests for 64 things ! Someone must be disappointed ! In the past thirty years I've waited at odd times in odd places, often for hours and obtained the autograph of Noël Coward. Never introduced myself. Just queued with his other admirers until it was my turn. Said please and thank you. Got a pleasant smile and was obliged with his autograph – the world's most swopable ! Well, in Diary 3, I mentioned this fact. Now, the 107th has asked for one. There are none left ! They are all swopped !

And this will amuse Mr Coward (if he ever reads it). Four signatures of Noël Coward torn from four pages of albums got me the authentic genuine and superb autograph of W. Harrison Ainsworth. I am so sure Mr Coward will agree that four of his *are* worth one of Mr Ainsworth !

On the other hand, I was offered *ten* Diana Dors signatures for one Mr Coward autograph, and turned it down ! Will this displease the delectable, desirable Diana ? What happened to the other sixty ? Five I gave away at *no* swops at all, in goodwill. But they were to such nice people who really and truly were Noël's fans – but just that too shy to ask him themselves. The rest went in exchange for such autographs as Jack Dempsey's, Miss A. Christie, H. G. Wells all of which I'd lost in the blitz. My surplus Coward signatures replaced one by one the signatures that went up in the 1941 blitz.

The government gave me *no* compensation at all for a glorious cigarette card collection, or my burnt albums of autographs (so much for the Lord Mayor of London Fund – I made four applications and all ignored. I lost £200, but the lousy British government civil servants gave me not even two pence !). But now, aided by the world's most swoppable autograph, I have been able to get back nearly all the signatures I was not able to get in person.

It's a strange and wonderful world – and in this world autograph collecting is the friendliest hobby. I have no more 'swops'. I have no more duplicates, I now have 11,201 different autographs – and I'll give the lot away to the B.M. the day I get the signature of a really nice lady on Marriage Lines ! Golly, Ive just realised the British Museum would be to some extent the Government ! Blimey, you can see me giving them or civil servants *anything* ! It seems I must make a will. And I *will* – will make a will willingly – when I've something to will. I will leave my autograph collection to Noël Coward so that he can sell it and send the entire proceeds to the actors orphanage.

Is it worth it ? January 1958

I have this night lectured in a bitterly cold hall to a cold group of middle-aged women in Bishops Stortford. I had to fight for a few minor smiles and I trembled with the cold. I started talking at ten to eight and finished at five to nine. I got to the station at three minutes past nine, to find *next* train to London was 10.22 ! ! Only two trains home to London at night – 8.22 and 10.22. Aint it a god-forsaken hole ! The snow was falling. I was perished. I got to London too late for a bus and had to have a taxi. The taxi man charged *double*. I felt too whacked-out to argue with the swine. I didn't make 20 bob on the whole 'do'. Is it worth it ? I wonder what Mr Gilbert Harding would have done ? Probably not gone in the first place – he's got sense. Me, I'm potty !

The World is small. January 1958

For some six months Ive had an ardent admirer of my writings out in Estoril, which is in Portugal. Hearing from Noël Coward on Broadway that he was going to keep his word and edit Diary Four I mentioned this fact to my never seen, one and only Portuguese resident reader ; and low and behold he sent me a cablegram that he had recently had from Mr Coward, and explained in a letter that Noël calls him Tremble Toes because his hands shake. Now how was I to know that a man in Estoril is a close and old friend of Noël Coward ?

Incidently he ordered six copies of it (No.4) the first order I had and I havnt yet completed a fifth of the book. I must get a move on. . .

And yet going through diaries covering the past forty years is a long job, for I have to edit them carefully so that they dont contain what I like but what will delight everyone else in Estoril, Timbuctoo and Pio Pio. Indeed, what makes me sweat is that I am writing a book for Noël Coward ! This is the height of my fame. I will *never* go higher. Its the *final Diary*. I am alone in this world so what is the use of working so hard ?

January 1958

I've just learnt with a good deal of interest that whereas we have in England the Angry Young Men (and women) they now have in America a similar group of young folks who are called the BEATS and to be a 'beat' in, say San Francisco, is the same (if not worse) as being an Angry Young Man in Chelsea. I have to record this because it seems that when ever possible in U S A they – the beats – get *dope*. God, what silly fools they are ! Do they really think that theres any dope in this world that aids creation ?

I can recall quite angry young men in the late 1920's but credit must be given they really *did* create novels stories, plays, poems, and some obscure (to me) forms of painting and sculpture. They worked ! They worked the anger out of themselves. My information from U.S.A. says the 'Beats' create nothing. They have a way of life and its an extremely depressing way – and a morbid one. And this is the future generation of America – or at least some part of it. Oh, I do hope someone will beat some sense into the 'Beats' before it becomes too late !

From my Fan Mail. January 1958

Or ri', Fred Bison, me old brahn son, ere's me arf a bar an' a tanner, so please send me yer Third Dahry. There's Pepys & Evelyn & Greville an' them there, but give me Bison, 'e's the bloke what knocks 'em from Westmoreland Road all the w'y to 'ere.

HENRY BENNETT
Room 1611
Carteret Hotel
208 West 23rd Street,
New York 11, N.Y.

Hertford College
Oxford
18 Jan 58

Dear Mr Bason,

. . . In I think it was the 1948 edition of *The Saturday Book* you referred to a man in Berkshire who was a toilet paper collector. This interested me especially as I am a member of a small group at this university who indulge in this hobby, and so I wonder if you could tell me anything which might lead me into contact with this man, or anyone else you may have heard of who collects toilet paper.

Yours faithfully,
EAN WOOD
(Pronounced 'Ian')

P.S. How many autographs have you got now ?

Thought for today. January 1958

Men dig deep into the earth and obtain oil – then men dig deep into the earth to make shelters to protect them from the missiles the oil drives to our destruction.

19th February 1958

Its just 30 years ago today that speedway racing came from Australia and the very first public meeting was at High Beach, near Epping Forest. Its grown and grown these 30 years but strange to say I've never been to a meeting of speedway – although I once got the autograph of a speedway king named, I believe, Wal Phillips (I'd have to hunt through 150 vols to find if this is his name but I'm pretty sure it is). Why have I missed this sport ? It just doesn't appeal to me at all. But then neither does motor racing. I've never been to a motor race as I refuse to pay to see men go round and round like a glorified merry go round as they thumb their noses at injury or death.

A Sudden Thought at 2 in the morning on a sleepless night. February 22nd, 1958

Who can really say for sure wether man makes life or wether life makes a man ? Are events or only thoughts (and plans) the powerfull agents of life ? There is never a life story that is really a life story – the inner thoughts are never revealed in any published life, and its these thoughts which become plans that make for events – or lack of events. So we come back to the first query that I cannot solve – does man make life – or is it life and the way its lived that makes the man ?

And now having gone round in a circle I will count sheep and get some sleep . . . I wish a really nice woman was in bed with me now. To hell with blooming sheep !

February 1958

The death of Charles Morgan brings to mind the fact that publishers *do* at times pass over good things when they are right in front of their noses, because Morgan's *Portrait in a Mirrow* was rejected by twenty five publishers before it was accepted. Finally it went into four editions and won two very good literary prizes !

I once met C. Morgan, it was more than 20 years ago. He was standing outside the New Theatre with his wife Hilda Vaughan. I had a sack of books on my back and looked grubby and shabby, for I'd been out book hunting, and one doesnt hunt in ones best clothes.

I took off my cap and said to Mr Morgan : 'Do allow me to congratulate you on your very clever novel *The Fountain*. May it spurt royalties for you for many years. Its a *very* good novel.'

He actually BLUSHED. He said it was the nicest compliment that had been paid to him in years. He asked who I was and I said merely a seller of books, and he said 'not *merely* . . . where would writers be if there were no booksellers? May a fountain of good books forever sprinkle your way!'

Marie Lloyd. Written May 1958 on a dull Sunday

Week after week music halls are closing down, and I think that the next generation will be asking What *was* a music hall? Even today in 1958 its almost a curiosity to see a *real* old time variety bill, except on television, where its put on almost as a period piece. Its all very sad. Some of the happiest evenings of my life have been spent in variety houses up and down the country, and even this day I myself would very much sooner see a good music hall show from the gallery than *My Fair Lady* from the stalls! When there are no more music halls there will be a big gap in my life and, I will declare in the lives of many other people.

The first time I ever went to a music hall was on a very memorable occasion, for it was in February of 1920, on the day that Marie Lloyd was FIFTY. She was appearing at The Bedford Music Hall in Camden Town. The Bedford was a very very famous variety theatre and all the real stars appeared there at one time or another. Alas, its now no more a theatre. My father had been able to do a kindness to Marie Lloyds chauffeur at a time when he was suddenly taken ill one night, and this man later gave my dad a couple of tickets to attend a historic night in Variety history – the greatest of all music hall stars *greatest* night.

Its strange to record that it was not only my own first attendance at such a theatre but the first time my father had visited such a place either. My dad was a dry old stick, and visited the theatre *six* times in seventy years of life, besides going less than a dozen times to a cinema. And he never read a novel in all his life. Just before he died he told me that he had only read through ONE book in all his life; that was *Robinson Crusoe,* which was given to him as a school prize in the year 1878 and which he left to me together with the rest of his earthly possessions – which consisted of 14s. 9d. in cash, a pair of cheap cuff links, a silver watch that hadn't gone for twenty five years and an Edwardian tiepin ! Ive spent the 14s. 9d. long ago as I bought a 15s. wreath for his coffin, but I still have the other things.

It was a long journey from Walworth to Camden Town ; we went both by tram car and bus, and it took more than an hour. Our seats were in the third row of the stalls, for the second house. The first house was at six fifteen, and the second house just before nine. The whole place was packed. There wasnt a seat *anywhere* vacant.

I recall some of the bill. It started with two dancers and followed with a juggler. I remember this was the first time I saw a man juggle with three cigar boxes. Ive tried a hundred times since that evening to do the same trick and always failed and smashed dozens of boxes in my vain attempts. And it looked so *very* easy in 1920.

I remember very well that during the interval after six acts had been on my father treated me to two pennyworth of pease pudding and a savaloy. There wasnt such a thing as ice cream or lollypops. The pease pudding was brilliant yellow and was dished out from a large square tin with a big wooden spoon and smacked out on a small piece of white paper, size about five inches square. The pudding overwhelmed the bit of white paper, but there was a lump of newspaper to help hold it. The savaloy, which was a little thicker and a little redder than todays sausages, was stuck on the extreme top of the pudding. This was a full blow out meal, and I mean blow out. It took me all through the interval and way into the second half of the programme before I had finished my two pence worth.

My dad had two savaloys between two large hunks of bread, and this was three pence. There was lots and lots of wollop to be had, but my dad was all his life a tee totaler. Never once in over seventy years did he take an alcohiclic drink. I once asked him why, and he said he was too poor to have it when he felt inclined to have it, and having got used to going without it, got out of what others made a habit of. He enjoyed ginger beer ; it made him beltch but he enjoyed it. He had ginger beer from a stone ware bottle as he sat enjoying the show, and he gave me some sips from it to help down my pease pudding.

We had a very good time of it, and what's more pretty nearly everyone around us was doing the same thing, eating and drinking – yes, whilest the show was on ! Untill the star of the evening came on. It was Marie Lloyd and this day was her fiftieth birthday. And I must confess that she looked fat and fifty, but then I was only thirteen and at my age everyone over 45 looked ancient and three parts in their grave.

Marie Lloyd was on that stage for around twenty five minutes, maybe a bit more, and she sang five songs and then three encores and then a second chorus of the final encore, and most of the audience joined in every song except me and me Dad. I only knew two of her songs : One of the ruins that Cromwell knocked about a bit, and another about An old cock linnet. The most popular song she sang that memorable night was one called A Little of what you fancy does you Good.

Having been brought up and lived always in a very tough Cockney district of London, I was every much a Cockney as Marie and I knew by her winks nods and shrugs just like everyone else just what she was singing out. She was a real saucy piece. She was not a big woman, not big like Kate Carney who was another music hall star of her period, not big like Florrie Forde, who was a tall and strapping wench. I doubt if Marie Lloyd was more than five foot two. No doubt in her 20s she'd been a smasher, and even at fifty she held herself very well and was nifty on her feet. She couldn't sing, not like what they sing at Covent Garden; she didnt have a singing voice, but just sort of said it to some sort of tune, but you could hear every word.

Between 1920 and 1922 when she died I heard her six times and I met her in person twice. They were the swan song years of a very hectic life, and I would say that she wore very well indeed, although in the last year 1922 she was very very ill and carried on when she ought to have been in bed. She died in harness. She collapsed on the stage of the Edmonton Empire, now a forgotten house of variety. The audience thought that she was 'kiddin' as she was reeling around like an old drunk, but she was dying on her feet !

She had a very wonderfull courage and a heart of gold. There was never and there never will be a more generous woman in the whole history of the Theatre and she was also one of the greatest artists who ever stepped on any stage. Her facial expressions were wonderfull and she could put a wealth of meaning into a wink. To say that Marie Lloyd was vulgar was utterly untrue. She could make black white and the gutter became the pavement. She was all London rolled into one very wonderfull lady, and that night when first I saw her the entire stage was covered with masses of flowers at the close of her performance. Hundreds and hundreds of pounds of glorious flowers. Never in 30 years since that day have I witnessed such homage to a Queen of the Halls or such cheering for a STAR. And when she made a little speech of this being the happiest day in her life, you knew – everyone knew – she *ment* it.

I didnt get her autograph on this occasion, because there were HUNDREDS at the stage door. It would have been absolutely impossible, but it was very nearly midnight before we left The Bedford and a lot past one o'clock when my dad and me got home.

Marie Lloyd sang as one of her favourite numbers 'Youre a thing of the past old dear'. Yes, that was the title.

They *had* titles like that thirty years ago. Another of her songs was 'Everybody wondered HOW he knew what he knew'.

Today Marie Lloyd is a name of the past, and alas so are Music Halls, and if you wonder how I know what happened more than thirty years ago, its so easy to explain. Before I went to sleep that night when I was 13, I wrote it all down, and started keeping a diary, and now today I can bring back a memory to mind with just a few notes and a programme.

Its most strange to record that I was sixteen when I met a not very well known man named James Agate. He was an *ardent* admirer of Marie Lloyd. She was the greatest star he'd ever seen, except Old Lady Sarah Bernhardt – who was more like a plague and pest in his life and haunted him.

This year (1958) fans mobbed Tommy Steele. 30 years ago I saw fans Mob Marie Lloyd. My God, what *worlds* between them ! And what a great difference between these 2 cockney stars !

On Baron Corvo. 1958

A young bookseller named Victor Hall came to see me yesterday when I was very busy. I stopped work and entertained him for he was genuine about his admiration for my diaries and this is a thing which SELDOM happens. I get more kicks up my pants from fellow booksellers than any other group in the world. Indeed, to get a kind word from a bookseller always astounds me !

During the course of our conversation we got talking about that eccentric genius Frederick William Rolfe alias Baron Corvo. I have not had many copies of his writings. The demand from America for his books far far exceeds the supply and every bookseller is on the alert for not only first editions but ALL editions. The most profitable bit of Corvo business Ive yet done was by sheer chance to find a copy of *The Wide World Magazine* with an article by Corvo in it about how he was buried alive. I knew several men who would probally like this minor item. I offered it to one. He had already got it, three times over, so I went further up the same road and offered it to another collector. He jumped with joy ; he'd never seen a copy. Mark you, he lived in the same road as the man who had it three times over. I said that I would accept his fairest offer. After all he knew what it was worth to him and he made an offer. It was very generous and I took it at once, and me and Lizzie had a charbanc trip to SOUTHEND on the proceeds, which was most delightfull, for like James Agate I like Southend.

I learnt that Victor Hall has made an intense study over the past seven or eight years into the life and the writings of Baron Corvo and counts himself amongst the Barons most fervent admirers. I must record the fact that I found Hall's account of his own quest for the books of Corvo very fascinating. I did much the same questing over 25 years ago for the books of Maugham. On the occasion of his call on me he was particularly elated because that very day he had come upon a copy of Cecil Woolfs Bibliography of the works of Corvo, which he said was a mine of information for all Corvinists, and a model of what a Bibliography should be, but rarely is.

I thought that this was a dig at me for my own Maugham Bibliography which was published in 1931, and I had to defend myself by saying that NO one, no one at all gave me any help when I compiled that Bibliography, and every one who could have given me some pointers and guides to the various issues and variations of first editions refused. Yet when my work was published they immediately condemned it, because it had three minor errors. Still, as I told Hall, the entire edition was SOLD OUT in less than six months, and now to find a copy is a sight for sore eyes.

I was most interested to learn what must be exclusive news and so *must* go into a diary : that a man named A. T. Bartholomew was really the first person ever to attempt a serious bibliography of the writings of Corvo together with a biography. This happened some time before the great Sir Shane Leslie and A. J. A. Symons either put pen to paper in this connection. Unfortunately Mr Bartholomew died before he was able to complete his work, although his m.s.s. still survives. I call this very interesting news indeed. Maybe there is a Mrs B. who will let the world read of her husband's studies. I never get tired of reading about Corvo, and that is the truth.

There has always been and I am very sure that there always will be an air of mystery surrounding Frederick Rolfe. Some of his writings are very very bald, not to say downright indecent, but then Corvo was in his way a genius.

Here's another genius for you. I feel that James Joyce first editions, now being rather neglected, will also prove to be good investments for the future. I hope that I am not wrong. I *have* been wrong. I burnt my fingers and my bank account long years ago when I made a corner in the first editions of Martin Armstrong, and lost fifty percent of my investment when Armstrongs writings were not being collected. But I am very sure that it will not happen with either Corvo or James Joyce. For one sure thing is that there are not enough copies to go round.

I have to end this days diary with a bit of information. I am told that in the year 2000 there will be three men to every woman in the world. What a blessing I will be O U T of it by then. Its such a horrible thought.

Ever so Wilde. 1958

Now for a tale which concerns my invaluable landlady. The Rector of Bloomsbury happens to be one of my fans and two years ago he sent me congratulations on my latest Diary together with a most interesting letter from Oscar Wilde as a Christmas gift. It was most generous of him and as I did not possess Wilde's autograph I was extremely excited. I rushed down to the kitchen and said to Lizzie

'Oh look ! I've had such a lovely present. A Vicar has sent me Wilde's autograph. It's a real treasure.'

Lizzie said 'Wilde's autograph ! Cor luv a duck. He ain't so much to get excited about. Why, my brother Bert knew him very well. My brother Bert had a drink with him on lots of occasions. My brother Bert could have got it for you as easy as kissing your hand. Wilde ! Cor, I don't call him a treasure. Smart, clever – oh yes, but *not* a treasure.'

'But it is a treasure. Wilde is dead. Your brother couldn't get him *now*, anyway.'

'Oh, poor man. Didn't know he was dead. Had a lovely left hand – and his right ! Cor, smart – he was dynamite. A champion.'

Well, I hadn't heard no one call Wilde dynamite before.

I said to her 'Wilde died broken-hearted after coming out of prison.'

'What, that nice man in prison ? Poor man. What a right hand he had. Bang, and down they went ! Didn't get up again. Bang. Best knockout. Yes, Wilde was a knockout he was an all !'

'Here, Liz, who are you talking about ?'

'Wilde, Little Jimmy Wilde. My brother knew him quite well.'

'I'm talking about *Oscar* Wilde.'

'Who's he ? Jimmy's brother ?'

'No, he wasn't any relation whatsoever. Oscar was a writer.'

'Oh – a writer like you ?'

'No, Lizzie dear, not *quite* like me.'

'Well, he couldn't be, could he, not *quite* like you.'

And having reached complete agreement I went back to my study somewhat shaken.

This is short and sweet. It is also true. I know a bloke who collects antique pottery and china. He's a working class chap with rather expensive tastes. He looks for bargains, and so often gets them. Well, this here bloke went into a shop in one of the back streets of Brighton and asked the price of a quaint bust of Nelson. The owner said the price of it was 10s. and 6d. The bloke whistled with surprise and said 'By Golly ! That's expensive. Very expensive seeing as how its only got one arm !' And the owner of the shop looked at it and said 'Dear me, so it has. I hadn't noticed one arm was missing. You can have it for 5s.'

The Books in my own special Bookcase at the age of sixteen

1. *Swiss Family Robinson.* My first 'favourite' book.
2. *The Adventures of Sherlock Holmes.*
3. *Liza of Lambeth.*
4. *Pears Encyclopaedia.*
5. *The Art of Boxing* by Tommy Burns, ex world champion.
6. *Bits from an old Bookshop,* A Bookseller's Memories.
7. *Barlasch of The Guard* by Seton Merriman.
8. 3 battered copies of *Chamber's Journal.*
9. An early volume of *The Strand Magazine.*
10. A rather good guide to London with illustrations.
11. Walker's *English Dictionary.*
12. *The Worlds Wit and Humour,* Volume 5. American book of 1906.
13. *Hide and Seek* by Wilkie Collins.
14. *King Solomons Mines.*
15. A pocket Doctor and Medical Dictionary.

No matter what I sold, I never let it affect this row of books. They were my company on many lonely evenings – and never let me down.

The Books in my own special little bookcase in my study at the age of 46

1. *Of Human Bondage* (with an intimate inscription from Maugham to me).
2. *Cavalcade of Song* – 50 years of songs. Introd. C. B. Cochran.
3. *Robinson Crusoe* (once owned by my father).
4. *Pepys Diary*. A cheap and battered edition.
5. James Agate's *Shorter Ego*, Vols. 1 and 2.
6. B. R. Haydons *Journal*. Very worn out.
7. Oscar Wilde's Works (falling to bits).
8. *Shake Hands and Come out Fighting* by L. A. G. Strong
9. *Those Foolish Things* by M. Sadlier. Nice USA edition.
10. *Chelsea Buns* by Noël Coward (Anon.) 1924.*
11. *Pears Encyclopaedia.*
12. *A Book of Blokes* by Sir W. Nicolson.
13. Funk & Wagners Dictionary.

Can you tell a man by his books ?

A list of my favourites. 1958

Favourite comedians	Bernard Miles, Benny Hill, Charlie Drake
Favourite actors	Alec Clunes, John Gielgud, Alec Guinness
Favourite TV personality	Cliff Michelmore
Favourite dancers	B. Grey, M. Fonteyn, John Gilpin
Favourite actresses	Flora Robson, Peggy Ashcroft, Diana Wynyard

* Given to Noël Coward in 1958 as a gift on hearing that he hadn't got it.

Favourite future stars	Margaret Anderson and Daphne Slater of TV
Favourite playwrights	Noël Coward, T. Rattigan, Benn Levy
Favourite dream	Just one month in America, to give some lectures and meet some wonderfull friends. Oh and of course female company
Favourite newspaper folks	Nancy Spain, Arthur Helliwell, Alistair Cooke
My favourite show	*Bitter Sweet*
Favourite magazine	*Esquire*
Favourite authors (as people)	(That's a tough one.) Grahame Greene, Neil Bell, Naomi Jacob
Favourite entertainer	Larry Adler (in class all on his own)
Favourite and happiest meeting of my life	Meeting Stanley Rubinstein my lawyer friend
Favourite novels	(Another tough choice.) *King Solomans Mines. Sorrell and Son* (W. Deeping) and *Of Human Bondage* (Maugham). *London Belongs To Me* (Norman Collins)
Favourite people I would like to meet	Lord Beaverbrook, Douglas Fairbanks, Billy Butlin, Ingrid Bergman
Favourite ambition	Well, of course, its still to find one *decent* English lady who doesn't think an author is 'very odd', that reading is 'a waste of time', or that I am a freak. Who will share my eventfull life and its ups and downs. I promise her loyalty, utter

	faithfullness and very very seldom dull days, in return for just *sheer kindness* !
Favourite city in England	Southend (it used to be Eastbourne)
And for what it is worth my most disliked place	Inverness, in the hard frozen north

And now some of my dislikes. Malcolm Muggeridge is a dislike. Established English civil servants get me down ! Starletts of the screen who only shine in *bed* or at first nights, they get me down ! Oldham on a wet foggy night, thats a dislike ! Manchester on a winters afternoon, raining of course – that gets me down ! I loathe the ever increasing Honours List, of O.B.E. for heaven knows why reasons, knights of the stage. *Some* of them get me down. Very snobbish cricketters get me down. These are some – oh, I will admit somewhat petty but *honest* – dislikes of mine.

I do not apologise for having a few dislikes. I *know* my enemies. I also know my friends. I have a great deal more friends than enemies and thats always a very good thing, unless you happen to have the mind of a Baron Corvo and then you go out of your way to make people *hate* the sight of you. That Ive never *knowingly* done in all my life. On the other hand I have for ever refused to 'put on an act' in order to win favour. Hell to that lark. *To beg Id be very ashamed* ! ! I dislike people who write asking favours yet do *not* send s.a.e. I must admit I *do* like Lady Docker although I've never spoken to her – at least she is always herself ! I do *not* like 'PUNCH'. It is a very cruel magazine – unless you are *extremely* powerfull ! I do not like folks who really do earn 40,000 to 60,000 a year yet *grumble* when the bloodsuckers take 19s. 6d. in the pound. Why the hell dont they earn *less* ! And to those who grumble about taxes I have a lovely slogan – If you cant take it with you Dont Go !

On Having completed 35 years of keeping a diary. 1958

I have always had a great admiration for the diariest Benjamin Haydon, and I believe that his autobiography and journals had a good deal of influence on my life, especially at the beginning. I had keepted a rather untidy diary at the age of from eleven, but I got more in my stride and more like a real diarist around the age of 15, for by then I was a very ardent collector of autographs and had to put into diary who I met, what they had to say to me, how they were dressed and wether they were amiable folks. I had also to put appointments and tentative dates of places where I hoped to meet the stars, and a record of first nights and of the opening of this and that, where there was likely to be a celebrity. It was essential to have a diary, and without it I would have been lost.

And now today, 35 years latter, I would still be entirely lost without my diary at my side. I have now an appointment book, and an engagement calendar. I seldom these days put dates or appointments into the actual diary, but try to recall, as soon as possible after the event, just what happened, and at a rough guess 75 per cent of the things I now write up are in a humerous vein. I was recently asked at a lecture why I keepted a diary. There were many answers that I could have given : sheer egoism; as a record of my joy in living; that there is a very grave waste of good if we dont preserve experience; to aid my memory in my old age so that I can recapture the thrills of long ago.

I am reminded of a part from Ben Haydons work. It reads – I quote – 'I acquired in early life a great love of the journals of others and Johnson's recommendation to keep them honestly I always bore in mind. I have kept one for 34 years. It is a history, in fact, of my mind. I hope that my journals, if ever they are thought worthy of publication, may give as much pleasure to others as other journals have given delight to me.' End of quote.

I dont think I could put it in a better way than Ben did. I was quite inspired by his work, and of course, Pepys work, as well. A chat long ago with James Agate – 'keep a diary and some day it may keep you' – only made me more enthusiastic, and caused me to weed and become a little more choosey in what I put into them. I can honestly say that I never never thought that they would be published, and they most certainly would not have been but for Nicolas Bentley. I never offered them for publication ! I was quite contented to go to my journals and diaries when I found in time a need to write a small article or a radio script. From my notes I could for years have written 3000 word articles.

But when Nick asked to take the whole lot away and make a book of them I would have been darft to have refused, as here was the one chance of my life to be a PUBLISHED Diarist, a modern Samuel Pepys.

I improved in some way around the year 1933, when I had read my friend Arnold Bennetts journals. Some people have the silly idea that theres absolutely nothing in writing up a diary, any style does, and you can put anything in, even the weather or what you eat for breakfast, or wether you had a hangover. But its only when you have been 35 years at the happy task that you realise that even a diarist is an artist, mostly despised, but nevertheless in his *own* way a man of letters. . .

I am most happy. Happy Birthday. 35 years faithfull to my diaries. Its a pretty good record. And it doesn't matter to me if the world never sees this. What really matters is that I've been true to myself and keepted my word to myself. And I will end todays diary with a slogan. Play and be happy, then go back to work and be happy. Because you cant be happy for long without work.

Some things I've learnt in life. 1958

1. Never be seen speaking to any policeman.
2. Avoid some civil servants as you would the plague.
3. Always let a woman have the last word.
4. Never argue with an editor or a producer on the fee you receive for work done.
5. Avoid tax trouble and the people in tax offices by earning just enough to avoid taxation. I do NOT mean evade it – just dont earn it.
6. *Never* believe that women are the weaker sex.
7. Take *no* notice of titles. Ive known *one* nice 'Lord'.
8. Never ever lend more than £2 to anyone at any time because by lending you lose the friendship of the borrower. In 10 years I have lent £24. I only got back £2 and I lost 12 friendly acquaintances.

Games played in my childhood days. 1958

When I was a school boy we played with peg-tops and hoops. We also played a jolly game called The Poor Horse. A boy would bend and lean against a wall supporting himself against it with his hands flat against the wall. When he said 'Ready' another boy would climb onto his back – and then another on his back – and another on *his* back – and so on. The neat idea was to see how many boys could climb on before the one underneath – the horse – collapsed. If he did not collapse and could take his hands off the wall and walk a couple of steps before they all slid off he was A Gallant Horse or A Bold Horse. If he couldnt move at all with say just 2 boys on his back he was A Poor Horse and the boys on his back were allowed one smack at his back side.

I soon learnt that I was not strong enough to carry even one boy unless he was a very little boy but I also learnt that a couple of copies of *The Gem* or some other paper of my childhood days was good enough protection except from a boot !

I haven't seen The Poor Horse played for all of 30 years. The last time I played it I was the 2nd on the horses back and number 3 came onto my back and I collapsed throwing the boy above me bang on to the pavement. But the strong boy underneath moved several paces with another boy and myself on his shoulders so no one got kicked, and I gave all my sweets to this strong boy. He was finalist in the A B A Middleweight championship later and but for his girl friend who did not care to see his 'lovely face' disfigured he would have turned pro and very likely have beaten Len Harvey – thats how good he was.

If anyone in Walworth refused to join in a game we did not blow him a raspberry or give him the bird. Our gang leader carried around with him a tin can which had threaded through the bottom of it a piece of string with rosin on it and by working the string with his fingers he could make a noise just like the cackle of chickens. And when he pulled this string and we heard the noise and called out 'Chicken hearted' the chap we called it to knew he was in disgrace and a coward and he had to do something really very brave to get back into the gang and our good books again – brave like breaking a window on purpose and then stand there and argue with the owner of the window that it was a sheer accident and get away with it without a clip round the face. Or stealing an apple from the front of a stall at the place where they were piled up so that when he removed the apple the rest fell down into the roadway as he run away. Yes, brave like that.

On the Death of James Stephens. 1958

He was a real nice little man, friendly amiable and very talkative. I dont think he had many enemies – even in the world of literature which is full of jealous and spiteful people. I dont think he was much above five foot, if that, but he radiated personality and good will. He had a large sized head and a large sized heart to match it. His face was very wrinkled and there were many many lines in his bald forehead. He often had a merry twinkle in his eyes, and you knew, of all Irishmen, he was one who *believed* in fairies and leprechauns!

He could tell a tall tale, and in the very manner of his telling it you knew that it wasn't tall to him. He could have made it much taller and *still* believed it. He was a very unpractical man and always willing to listen and even more willing to talk to all and sundry.

He came into fame via his noble book *The Crock of Gold*, and it became so very successfull that it brought to him a goodly amount of gold. The first time we met was in Broadcasting House. I was a very raw and nervous beginner. He put me at ease.

Our second meeting was in his own home in London, and there he said a piece of wisdom that I never forgot. I will now pass it on to you. James Stephens said:

'If, my boy, in the swan song of your life you can look back and say that you made six good loyal friends in your life, then you will indeed have been a very lucky man. Most people are lucky to make three good friends. Keep on searching; you may never find the end of the rainbow but the seeking for friends is a very worth while endeavour.'

He did not use quite these words but this was the meaning.

His delicate and fragile poems will be read as long as the world reads poems. The world was richer for James Stephens. He was a darlin man – a poet who believed in fairies.

Fantasticly true. 1958

The longer I live the more folks I know and the more tales they tell me. I have stored a few of the more fantastic up and feel they ought to have a place in my journals so that tellers of tall tales have the opportunity to say 'I can cap that ! Why, my goodness when I was in Poona in 83 . . .' Mark you, I dont care much for putting *third* hand stories into my books but when I tell you these tales came in conversation with really well known literary men then they deserve a record. Algernon Blackwood was the best teller of the spooky in my younger days but Montagu Summers and Clifford Bax were pretty nearly as good. I was assured these tales were *true*. True or not they are retellable and tall ! (Copyright owners, please forgive me!)

One is of an Indian who rather scoffed at the powers of a very wise old man he found in a forest. The old man claimed he was entirely free of both space and time. Perhaps the younger man had reasons to scoff at this astounding statement. He asked what would be the leading article in a certain newspaper tomorrow. The old man told him. The other man said that anyone could make such a hit or miss statement. '*Show* me tomorrows newspaper and I will believe you !'

Now it is a fact that those who are able to work miracles and wonders are most reluctant to do so. The old man meditated for a while – as if in a trance and then drew from some grass at his side *tomorrows* newspaper with the leader exactly as he had foretold. The young Indian was spell-bound with the wonder of this miracle and asked why the wise old man had proved his point and was told 'You will travel. You will travel far. Never forget that the world of the spirit is *ever* near you.' The young Indian returned the newspaper to the wise old man of the forest who made it disappear at once into nothingness.

When twenty hours later he saw that newspaper of that days date it was *exactly the same as the one he'd seen in the forest the day before* ! I think this is a lovely story and would make a really unusual film. The teller told me that *he believed it* !

And then theres the one which you'd have thought Guy du Maupassant had conjured up. Father and son were deeply attached to each other. The boy was not quite five and could not write much and did only just know his A B C. He had never attended school and was a rather delicate little boy. His father died suddenly. The little boy mopped. He was given pencil and paper to scribble on one afternoon 3 or 4 weeks after the death of his father and when his mother took away later on the scribble she found written in weirdly shaped but decipherable B O L D capital letters D E A R E S T W I F E I E. I am always at your side – today Tomorrow. Forever. Charlie. Her husband had always called her Wifeie. Unexplainable. The hard boiled will say some one wrote those words on the boys scribbling pad. But there was *no* one else in the house ! The mother did it in a trance ? Not really very likely. You can hardly comfort yourself with writing down what you already K N E W – and the lady was deeply religious. Montague Summers believed this utterly.

He also wrote in a letter to me another tale on the same lines about a widow who was in desperate circumstances. She had lost her husband by accident at a terribly grave period and was at her wits in for money. Her son was four. He had never been to school and quite unable to write even the simplest of words. The boy was scribbling as the mother was praying. The boy got up and presented his mother with a page of scribble. She stared at it. It seemed to be more like *shorthand* than actual scribble. Her husband had taught short hand as a side line. She herself was not able to read it. She took it to one of her late husband's former pupils. He found it difficult to decipher owing to being in a childish inexperienced hand – but he did in time decipher this shorthand and it told of money in a safe deposit in a town hundreds of miles away. Eventually she was able to get this money (a really considerable sum) and end the crisis. You would find it HARD to explain that tale ! Unless of course you care to say that the former pupil was in love with the widow, made up the safe deposit money and put some in the safe deposit for the lady he loved and then married her and his money. It could have been like that I suppose but somehow I do hope not !

And heres one that Rev. Montague Summers assured me was true. In a surburban district of London, there sat in a garden one summers afternoon a mother reading a novel. It was a peacefull pleasant scene. Suddenly one of her daughters leaned out of a 2nd story window to say that she'd done her piano lesson. The mother was just going to say something when she screamed as the window sash cords broke and the large window came down on her girl's head. The mother fainted at what seemed to her the gillotine fell. When neighbours came to help the mother and she recovered from the faint she was not able to move her arms and across both arms were raw weals as if a window had crushed down on them. The girl escaped entirely *unharmed* – being quicker than the fall of the window. But the mother was not able to use either of her arms for more than six months ! And for ever more carried the scars of her arms exactly as if the window had crushed down on them. Strange but true.

Seems to me this would make a theme for a really unsolvable murder mystery – mind over matter. Only I aint good at plots. And what about that young lady who dreamed of seeing a sad faced middleaged man 3 nights running in a dream. He beckoned to her – but somehow she refused to go towards him. 3 nights she saw this strange man to her vividly in a dream. The afternoon of the 4th day she saw the man in real life as he beckoned her to get on a train. She recalled her dream and her refusal to go to him – so she refused to board that train and the man in the role of a train guard got on it – and the train was involved in a terrible crash and 38 people died and 107 were badly injured. It happened ! Fantastic, oh yes, but L. A. G. Strong believed it.

I don't know who owns the copyright in these tales, but the men who told me them said I could re-tell them at any time.

It's a Business. 1958

Looking back on 30 and more years as a bookseller I can recall many times when I would have burnt my fingers and lost a goodly bit of capital if I'd dabbed a little too deep and above my humble station in the Book World. I lost a good deal of money in the de lux signed edition craze of the 1930's burning my fingers on first editions of Francis Brett Young and Martin Armstrong. I couldn't even get *cost* price after trying to make a small 'corner' in them !

This taught me a lesson I never forgot and I will put it down on paper. Never lock your money up in an author but only in a *book*. Buy for instance an attractive copy of one of R. Burns book of poems and you have a book. It may cost £200 but its a book and it would be extremely unlucky if you ever lost on this investment. Buy *King Solomons Mines, Treasure Island, Alice in Wonderland* – choose your own classic – and you'll have a book that will make a steady rise in value as each year goes by. But complete a set of the Works of Brett Young and you will burn your fingers (unless of course you are passionately fond of his novels in which case it wont matter a dam, as some pleasures you *have* to pay for).

If I was giving advice I would suggest for a *minor* investment to the tune of £100 that the *first* books of Yeats, De la Mare, James Joyce and T. S. Eliot would still be rather good to buy, and would make money providing you didn't pay the moon for them in the first place.

Personally, I've never found pleasure in book collecting. It has been my business and I never have hung on to a book. If I felt the price was right I took it. I never have cared what the other fellow got.

Of course, I've made countless mistakes. I sold a book once for 30s. and it resold for 40 pounds. Did it worry me ? Not a bit. But I wouldn't do it twice !

Very few rich men who own large libraries are *really* collectors of books – they are merely people who accumulate ! I've seen dozens of libraries where the books looked so nice but where there wasn't one book worth 10s. Had the rich man purchased instead the *first* novels of R. L. Stevenson, Maugham, Bennett and James Joyce he would have had more cash value in 4 vols than 400 on his shelves. Still, perhaps rich men dont worry over such things. Never being rich myself I dont know.

But to return to what I started to say on advice based on 30 years experience. I say never 'corner' a market in *one* authors books. You will regret it unless you happen to personally enjoy that author's books. As for a sad example I know a man who paid more than 150 pounds for a run of Galsworthy novels. 2 years ago he tried to resell them and was offered 5 pounds for the collection !

Sunday Morning in Walworth. 1958

One advantage of being ones own master and having a nice landlady is that you can get up at what time you like, and the day commences when you get up. As my day seldom starts until the postman arrives I invariably have a cup of tea in bed (Shame !) and get up about 8.30 – BUT the exception to this rule is Sunday mornings, for on that day I get up with the lark say at 7.45 and am out of my home, shaved and dressed *before* 8.30. (Oh yes, Lizzie has tea in Bed that morning !)

Sunday is a very very busy morning in my district of London (Walworth) and especially to me because that is when all the stalls and barrows come out in all their glory and the boys sell anything from pins to pictures. East Street and my own Westmoreland Rd are crowded with stalls and people from 8.30 a.m. till one and its very fortunate for all concerned that its not so well known as Petticoat Lane, or no one would be able to move at all !

I get about very speedily this Sunday morning as I rush from stall to stall to see what I can buy at a reasonable price which will enable me to get a small but honest profit. Altho I am a dealer in second hand books I do not find many books in Walworth (and in 29 years of seeking locally I have never yet found a rare book of *any* description), so I dabble in any thing from brass candlesticks and Toby jugs to ships-in-bottles and weird paintings.

It does not take me long to make up my mind over any of the goods offered for sale on the stalls and barrows and by 9.30 I have finished my morning buys and I am on my way back home for my cup of 'char' and I glance at the newspaper to find out who amongst the famous have 'pegged out' (in order to put a black border around their autograph in my collection of 11,171 autographs). This I call homage to them-that-obliged-me-when-living and now dead must be remembered with a black border ! Oh I know it sounds ODD. Alright, I'm odd – so what ?

At around eleven o clock I go out again for two reasons : the first to see if any fresh stalls have turned up and therefore any fresh bargains to offer; the second reason comes after business is over and I have spent all my 'investment money', for it is then I can linger at the stalls of the quack doctors, racing tipsters, fortune tellers and the like. With all these folk their stock in trade is 'the gift of the gab', the power to be able to convince you even *against your will* that black is white or off white ! I am fully aware that in my own small way I have something of this gift, but most of the Sunday Street Scene folks are my *masters* and from them I am able to take weekly lessons and have done so for the best part of twentyfive years !

Let me tell you about just two of them (since you are unlikely to brave the wilds of Walworth). Upon a stall, covered with a piece of white american-cloth, are laid out some surgical instruments which are or were at one time associated with child birth, fearsome shiny steel instruments of torture, and in tiny jars are said to be 'the seeds of children'. The stall holder put on his left hand side of the stall a pile of silver on a few pound notes, on his right side are pieces of what look like bark from a tree and roots from plants and there are also some hundred two inch square white cardboard boxes (under the stall is a suitcase containing more small boxes).

The quack has two 'stooges', men of middle age, neatly dressed, clean and tidy, and the Show opens. The quack holds above his head the largest of the child birth instruments and he shouts out in a very loud voice

'You *dont* know what you are talking about.'

'I do' says one stooge.

'Yes he does' says the second stooge.

'You dont' says the quack.

'I do.'

Then 'Rubbish !' and 'Fiddlesticks !' say the couple of stooges and low and behold the arguments have opened, and in five minutes there has gathered an audience ! The surgical things are waved around and the jars of 'children in bottles' are displayed to an awe struck crowd. It takes the man about twelve minutes in all to get down to what is in the little white boxes and what he is going to sell to MALE *adults only* ! Can you guess ? No, thats wrong. . . its nothing whatever to do with birth control, far from it, its rather the other way round !

In the heart of the West African jungle this man discovered on one of his numerous expeditions that the natives searched for the bark of a certain tree and the roots of a rare plant and ground the two items into a powder and when they needed *extra sexual vigour* they swallowed a dose and washed it down with pure crystal water, and they became men of vigour and were sought by women and ready for considerable whoopee. So if *you* are run down, getting tired of your wife, wake up sluggish, no clear glint in your eye, if, in fact, you have ceased to be a man and merely a wearer of trousers, then 'Buy a box of my magic pick-me-up.'

'It will, I give my word, fill you with desire, colour will be in your cheeks. You will eat well, sleep well and feel well. Two and six a box. I'm here every Sunday and if your wife is not astounded with your wonderful recovery by next week, if I have not brought to you the *extra* joy of life and renewed mans greatest gift within the next seven days, then come back here and with the same civility with which I now take your money, I will then have pleasure in returning your hard earned 2s. 6d. ! Here every Sunday when its fine. Here to help you. I am not hard up. Look, men, theres ten quid there ! Do I *need* your 2s. 6d. ? No ! But this magic potent comes all the way from West Africa and the cost is heavy. It has to be found; 2s. 6d. just pays the cost *only*. Try it, you'll be grateful to me. One for you, sir ? You had it before ?'

'Oh yes' says the stooge, 'its *remarkable* !'

'There you are gents, remarkable, he says, and it *is*, take my word. And one for you sir, and you, and you. . .'

He sells anything between 30 and 40 of the white boxes of powder at 2s. 6d. each time. Then he pleads for a rest and a smoke. The crowd melts away. Ten minutes later the Show starts all over again, with a duplicate dispute and the same waving of instruments and jars. Inside thirty minutes he sells another 20 to 30 boxes; between 9.30 and 12.45 he can sell *over 150 boxes* of the rare vigour stuff all the way from Africa.

In fact, a one time stall holder told me the man had been known to get rid of over 200 boxes on a fine morning, and taken £25 ! Not bad wages since he only works once a week. The stall costs 5s., the licence 1s. 3d. I dont suppose the stooges get more than £1 each, and thats good wages too for getting a crowd to gather. The boxes cost say 1d. each, I *dont* know where the powder comes from or what it contains, or whether it *does* what its said to do ! The quack is a big strong fat man, 14 stone of steel and muscle. I'd be a twirp to argue with him, and perhaps thats why Ive never seen a man go up and ask for his 2s. 6d. back, but he is a wonderful salesman and a master of his craft. I love to listen to him. Maybe one day when I have a wife and no vigour I'll invest 2s. 6d.

Then the second man I want to tell you of is a tipster, complete with jockey cap. He shows us bills (receipted) from hotels all over the country where he assures us that famous trainers and jockeys stay. He has a manner of implying that they *all* give him exclusive information. He has a racing car, which proves he doesnt need your money but is only there to help you with your racing, and the paltry 2s. he charges for his information merely pays for a few rounds of whiskies. But he often takes between £15 and £20 for his 'kind action' on Sunday mornings down in Walworth – and theres me, me, I consider I am lucky if I earn £4 a week. So I shall still listen and learn from him just *how* to hold a crowd with sheer 'gift of the gab'.

Last week he had a huge notice up. 'Just Pipped ! SWAN SONG. 33 to one. Hard Luck !' Now you'd think 'Just Pipped' ment that his selection got *2nd* beaten by a short head. Not a bit of it. This horse was 4th, 8 lengths from the winner ! (I went home to look it up.)

I was at one time a tipster myself, but only for greyhounds. I can still win 9 times out of 10 that I go to greyhound meetings, but I have ceased to advise anyone else. They swear at you when they lose and seldom say 'Thank you' when they win !

I love my Sunday mornings in Walworth. I have watched it for more than 30 years and what gifts I possess in the art of holding an audience come solely from listening to the masters of the Gift of the Gab down here in my part of London. I love Walworth !

March 1958

From *The Star* tonight I see that Paul Anka singing at the Slough Adelphi earns ten shillings a *second* – and he is 16. He is the highest paid boy singer in the world. I am tonight very willing to go to Slough and sing a whole SONG for 10s. Ive never know the book trade so bad in the past 20 years. One faint ray of sunshine the Croydon Federation of women write to say they are going to put me on their Rota from Nov. 1958. What on earth *for* ?

13th March 1958

Today I returned to BBC Womens Hour after a long silence. I had discided last year not to work hard or do more than 2 broadcasts a year and so avoid paying tax and helping to keep civil servants. The broadcast was an immense success. I was in great form and didn't stumble over a word. Coming out of the building after it I was still a little on edge and on top of the world. A middle aged lady standing just beside the entrance said 'Are you someone ?'

'What you mean Lady ? Of *course* I'm someone and Ive just been broadcasting ! My name is *Bason* !'

'Oh, is it ? I've never heard of you. Well, carry on with where you are going. I wont trouble you.'

So I went. I dont know what she might have troubled me for if she *had* known me !

31st March 1958

Some where there is a witness to this – but in any case its true. I caught the one clock train from Fenchurch St. to Westcliffe today to give a lecture. There was only one other person in my compartment and very soon he was chatting away to me (people usually do talk to me).

He started telling me his Life history (I didnt mind, he was a lonely old man) and he said that he was born in Kempston, near Bedford. I told him my mother was also born in that same village. He was interested but did not recall her maiden name, Blount. He then asked me if she was alive. I said no. He then said where did she die ? And at that *very second* I looked out of the window and we were at Hornchurch (not stopping) and I pointed out of the window and said, HERE ! And he asked what I ment and I said 'She died in Hornchurch Hospital, right here !' And added I will put this in my Diary tonight as an astounding coincidence. There are 30 stations on this line. There are 30,000 or more stations in Gt Britain – but that you should ask where did she die at the *exact* second we arrived and flashed through the town where she died is astounding. He agreed that it was ASTOUNDING !

17th April 1958

10 months ago this very week I sent Stephen Potter a magnificent photograph of himself well packed and with stamps for return, and the request that he honoured me by autographing it. Today I got a signed photo from Stephen Potter. *Not* the one I sent him, which was Mr Potter looking just like a forlorn undertaker. The one he's sent me has a smile on his face and looks as if he is a humourous writer – which he *is* ! I am well pleased.

I am also delighted to read this day from the writings of Casanova : 'The artifice which I employed was to recount the thing simply, and just as it was, without omitting even any circumstances which might be hurtfull to me. It is a secret which every man is not able to employ, because the greater part of the human race is composed of poltroons and to be always true needs courage. I have learnt by experience, that truth is a talisman of which charm never fails, provided that one does not squander it on rascals.' End of quote.

Funny how Ive missed this great piece of writing which I've lived up to the best of my ability in my writing and my lectures so many years. I always recount the thing simply, omitting nothing. Tonight I am on my way to Sheerness to talk to 80 or more middle-aged women. Willie says it sheer lunacy to go to Sheerness on a bitter cold damp night and all I will get is a cold. Ive pointed out that I might get a new friend as well, and that would be pleasant, whereas if I stay in Walworth I will never never know anyone in Sheerness ! So what ? Well, if I said No to all awkward lecture dates I'd very soon stop making new friends.

Later. I told the exact truth at Sheerness and I held them 46 minutes and they laughed 29 times. I sold 4 copies of my Diaries to strangers there. I don't know if I made a *friend* but I made a nice new acquaintance with a ship conscrution expert and I had a lovely tea actually in Sheerness Dockyard. And not everyone has a posh tea in a Dockyard, so all in all it was worth while and I've got no cold – yet !

18th April 1958

Today I got a request for a copy of *Lady Rose's Daughter* by Mrs Humphry Ward. Ive not had a copy in five years and the last copy I was glad to sell for 9d. after offering it on my lists at 1s. It would not be worth my while to go seeking another copy as any profit would be eat up by the fares.

It is interesting to record that over 50 years ago Mrs H. Ward sold the serial rights of this ever so dated novel (now) for 10 thousand pounds ! It also sold over 200,000 copies here and over 400,000 copies in U.S.A. and probably netted her twenty thousand pounds in all. Which is nice gravy *now* and was worth 10 times as much when the pound was worth a pound. It took her nearly nine months to write! Today, this lady is practically unknown, save to the very aged and no one under fifty would look at it or buy a copy even for 3d. It is strange that whereas Mrs Henry Wood continues to sell Mrs Humphry Ward is a Back Number! And if either were writing today Neither would, I'm pretty sure, find a publisher for their Novels.

How fashions change especially amongst the lady writers. Now I sell Doris Lessing, Rumer Godden, P.H. Johnson and Nancy Spain. Twenty years ago it was Ethel M. Dell and R. M. Ayres. Just how long will Rumer Godden and Doris Lessing be wanted? Will they either make a clear 20,000 pounds for a novel? I *do* hope so! I love to hear of people making good. I am really and truly pleasured when I see someone win the jackpot in a TV show. It is really true, my diary, that I do not envy anyone in all this world. I know I shall never make 20,000 pounds from *all* my work put together, but then I would not know what to do with such a sum. It would *worry* me.

Next Thursday I go to West Byfleet to talk an hour to a club and my fee is 21s. I will come home dead tired but if I have made many people laugh in that dull place where they dont yet know Mafaking has been relieved then I will have done a good job. If they paid 10 gns I would not work harder. The vicar there is a poor man and I know this 1 gn comes from his own pocket. Why should I impose? I will get the bigger fee where they can afford it (in the North). I wonder if I will be allowed to inspire someone in West Byfleet to write a novel and get 10,000 pounds for the serial rights of it? I hope so!

1958

She was my hostess after a Women's Institute talk. She looked quite a starchy dame with a grand manner until, when I asked for the W.C., she said 'Mention my name and you'll get a good seat !'

26th April 1958

I expect people will think I've joined the cat loving James Mason, G. Winn, Beverly Nichols group of blokes if they know that I am down right sad. We had to have Tibby, our little black and white cat, killed today. It had had a skin disease for 3 weeks and its fur was coming out in unsightly patches. We could see she was in pain. Lizzie took her to a vet and he said it was quite hopeless – nothing could cure our Tibby so Lizzie had her put to sleep. She gave the vet 1s.. We are sad today ! We MISS our cat.

May 1958

A very nice admirer in West Byfleet invites me to tea Oct 9th (when I return to lecture there) and has said in her letter 'We will have strawberry jam *especially* for you – and as much as you like !'

Now I wonder if I've told her or anyone else for that matter that once I had tea with a very very rich man and woman at Eastbourne. The table was beautifully laid and the jam pot was incased in a solid silver urn affair so you couldnt see into the jam pot. I dug down and I came up with a nice lot of strawberry jam. I put it on my bread and I eat it. Then I started again and I was just dipping down again when the rich woman said,

'You had TWO strawberries on your last slice of bread. You'd better have plain bread now !'

Aint it nice to be Mr Coward ? May 1958

Letter this day from Noël Coward in which he says he will be in the South of France June 1st till July 31st. Then at the Dorchester Hotel, London, August 1st for quite a while. Aint it nice to be Mr Coward from Jamaica to South of

France – sunshine all the way ? If he's lucky he'll get sunshine in London in August as well. Only the astounding thing is that it's *not* the best weather month of the year. Facts tell us July is best, yet 90% of Londoners go away in August.

Me, I go away in June – but then I would be different. Over a great many years now I have consistently found by observation that there is more and better sunshine in June than in all the rest of the months in Southern England weather. You don't get red as a lobster, you dont have to queue to get a meal, the holiday resorts are never overcrowded – and in June most librarians will give you a little of their time for a chat. Ive made it a rule when I visit a fresh town to seek out the Chief Librarian at the Public Library. 90% of them are extremely nice men and women – only 10% are extremely stuffy pompuss and utterly unapprouchable !

Because I want to meet a Librarian doesnt mean that I wish to sell them one of my diaries, really it does'nt. I would be most happy in many cases to give them copies quite free, but then they look upon that as a bribe so that rules out one as a gift. No, diary, its got *nothing* to do with selling. Most Librarians are book lovers and I am one as well, hence we have a common interest. But the reason for calling is (one) to be civil and sociable and to show myself and (two) to get a list of booksellers in the district ! Its lots quicker (and better) to get a kind Librarian to compile a short list of sellers of books than walk miles and miles often in vain looking for bookshops.

Now for the first time ever I've put on paper why I like to visit Librarians. Harmless, isn't it ?

May 1958

Cor, dont it break your heart ! Do some readers read what they see – or only what they *think* they see ? Ive had a letter from a man named Harper in West Bromwich. He says 'I am a lover of Robert Burns poetry and I noticed on page 77 in your Number one Diary you say that you would have been very glad to get a copy of his work in 1912. I have one dated 1901.'

Then it goes on and on with discription of this *useless* book of Burns poems and what do I offer for it ? Not being utterly INSANE I *never* make offers !

Then I thought to myself, 'Robert Burns ? I've NEVER read Burns in all my Life. My diaries are truthful so why would I put Burns ? I'm *sure* I never wanted Burns in 1912 for then I was only FIVE years old ! So I took a lot of time and I scouted around for my first Diary to see what the hell I *did* write so long ago.

Cor – it makes you spit blood – it really does. This is what I put. Its dated 1937 and I have written (and its printed as I wrote it) : 'I had a little find yesterday paying only 3d for R Brookes *John Webster & The Elizabethan Drama*. It is published 1916. Bound in black buckram & has a tiny label (I *hate* labelled titles – so soon get torn). I did not find it of great interest to read but I had no trouble to get 12s. for it. I think its worth 21s. out of the trade. (Mine was sold to a first edition dealer.) I wish it had been R.B's poems (1911). I would have had a holiday on the proceeds as the slim crown 8vo (also with a label) is worth £15.'

Now, isn't it obvious I'm talking about Rupert Brookes Poems ? Where *does* Robert Burns come into it ? And if I date a subject 1937 I am *not* writing of 1911 – or it would be dated 1911. And if I plead for Brookes Poems 1st edition 1911 I do *not* want an obscure useless valueless edition of R. Burns Poems dated 1901. Now *do* I ?

Of course I've gotta be ever so polite to the man and tell him *ever* so politely just what he can do with his Book of Burns Poems if he can find room !

And me feeling downright ill and worn out and then I have to do all this to ease my mind and yet I knew it couldnt be Burns for I loathed Burns and *all* his writings ! Oh, I know I'm 'odd'. I dont care for Henry James or Thackeray either ! But at least I know it and say so !

May 1958

I've been asked by a newspaper to comment upon the fact that Tommy Steele, the rock and roll expert (once of my neighbouring district of Bermondsey) got injured when madly mobbed by 300 girls in Dundee. I made no comment and said all posh-like 'I have no comment to make !'

The bloke really thought I was starchy and putting on airs but really and truly I wasn't, diary. I can put it here why I refused to say anything. I did pretty much the same thing when I was in my teens. Whilest its true that I didnt pull the stars hair out or clothes off (I would have probally risked my life to protect my favourites) I did most certainly become part of hero worshipping mobs on about 6 occasions.

It so happens I was there on the spot with ten other fans waiting for a star, but by the time the star came *out* 10 had become 500 ! And I had to fight not to lose my place at the side of the stage door after waiting hours !

I recall such a mob the night I got Pauline Frederick, the film star, to sign my book. No one knows of her today but in my teens she was a great big star (sort of Ingrid Bergmann, only *much* better). Then I recall another mob when I 'captured' Pearl White, who was a serial queen of the cinema. There must have been 1,000 people pushing and fighting to get near her. She was a sensation. (I recall Max Wall in her Lyceum Show – which shows the years he has been on the stage.) And I remember 400 people fighting to get a better view of Ivor Novello when he appeared in *The Rat* at The Brixton Theatre. And how I got crushed against the wall and near died. I had to kick and scream before the mob would get back and release little six stone me ! And I remember a Noël Coward first night when there was a hero worshipping mob that very nearly caused serious injury to a lot of folks. Yes, I've stood hours and trembled with excitement as the star at last came out. Its been happening more or less all through stage and variety history and nothing will change it except mounted police and secret exits and a real disguise for the star.

I often feel that stars bring these things on themselves. A pair of glasses and a small drooping moustache and no one would recognise Tommy Steele. I remember J.B. Priestley changed the shape of his hat, put his glasses down to the end of his nose, turned up his coat collar and no one but me recognised him at The Cambridge Theatre years ago. 26 people waiting to see him. They all knew him by sight – but he walked by all of them. I let him go 50 yards, caught him up and captured him. Oh no, I've no comment on hero worshipping, except its DARFT ! But I did it just the same in my teens.

Covent Garden. 1958

Without consulting other diaries (and I am too ill to move) I think I've been ten times to Covent Garden Opera House so I do nothing to uphold the high salaries that taxpayers help to pay. The most startling thing that happened to me concerning this place is when a man in Istanbul (Turkey) who was on his way home to New York City and stopped off in London for a matter of 24 hours. He wanted to see two things only – BALLET and BASON. He went to the box office and found that it was a M. Fontayn night and there was not a seat to be had at any price. (He was a rich oil man.) So he said to the man in the box office, 'Well, that's one of my dreams gone. Do you happen to know where a Cockney author named Fred Bason lives ? And the man in the box office immediately advised him and the quickest and best way to get to me and even wrote down the name of the road. Although to that date I'd never even *seen* that box office as all my seats were 'perks'. And the man from Istanbul walked all down my road and asked a dozen people where I lived. Then he happened to meet up with Lizzie who had just popped out to get some milk. She brought him home with her and we all had a merry 2 hours of conversation. That I call remarkably curious, knowledgeable and kind of Covent Garden box office staff.

The second occasion worth remembering was when I passed through the stage door entrance into the dressing room of a star. I was invited in by the star so the stage door man could not prevent me, although to show his power he did try. I had a ballet favourite Tamara Toumanova. As she appears so seldom in London it would be foolish to list her as my favourite dancer but she is *superb*. Well, I rather casually asked (without little hope) for a photo of her some dismal evening, and low and behold she invited me into her room to get it and have it signed personally to me.

She seemed utterly astounded that I hoped Mr Robinson was well. Mr R. was her husband. I had no idea she'd divorced him just awhile before our meeting. I spoke of the feeling that I would be a huge novelty in U.S.A. on TV and that my tales of Sinclair Lewis, Hemingway, Jolson, The Marx Brothers and 50 other stories would stagger TV audiences. She explained that Mr Robinson would not have been the slightest use to me; that he was *never* a discoverer of talent. She suggested Bennet Cerf, Alister Cooke and even Ed Sullivan as men with power who can help to make a newcomer in N.Y. City (even if they cant break him) rise into real stardom.

Having got a superb signed photo I departed from Tamara. (She had a terrible cough; she said the rosin on the floor caused that cough and it was almost an occupational disease with her.) She could not have been kinder or more thoughtfull and she made me an admirer for life. I spent 3 days later *twice* as much as I could afford on a seat at the Ballet just to watch Tamara !

I suppose I am glad The Covent Garden Opera House is there. In one hundred years Covent Garden has given a great deal of pleasure. Oh, on the day I was born Tettrazini was singing there. Thats what is called the department of entirely useless FACTS !

18th May 1958

I have been most awfully ill the past 2 weeks with what my doctor calls anxiety neuroses and depression and strain. I've overworked. I've been trying so desperately to complete Diary 4. With N. Coward as my editor I have to choose what I *hope* suits him. *No* one else matters. I have only to please Mr Coward and I've over worked and now I cant walk 10 yards without a blackout and I can only work ½ hr at the time and then rest 2 hours or so for I get terrific head and neck pains.

Well, having gone 2 successive weeks to the doctors at the exact same time I've seen the same people waiting in the same seats. I spoke to one of them about the extreme cold weather (I've never known a colder May) and then I said, 'I didn't see you last Tuesday.' And she said, 'No – I felt *much* too ill to come and see the Doctor !' That amused me.

19th May 1958

Another page in the book of life has turned, another gap in the days of my youth took place today with the death of Ronald Coleman in Santa Barbara at the age of 67.

I will never forget his great acting in the films *Lost Horizon, Beau Geste* and *A Double Life*. He was a very modest and extreemly gentlemanly man. Never in thirty years did I ever hear an unkind word said about Mr Coleman !

Its ever so strange to record that I got his autograph in a public lavatory. It happened that I spotted Ronald Coleman on one of his London visits. He came up from a lavatory and then I politely asked for his autograph. He said 'with pleasure, but its very public here.' Then he laughed and said : 'We will go down there' and nodded to the steps he had just come up. Mr Coleman sat down at the tiny desk in the attendents cubby hole and surrounded by toilet paper and white towels he signed my book. Then he made me promise not to tell anyone that he was in London, and no one that he had given me his autograph. I asked why he'd been so kind to me, and he said 'You touched your cap. A little politeness must always be rewarded.'

Then he added : 'And of course *never* say where I was when I signed your book. . . that would never do, would it ?' But now that he has passed on it dont do no harm to record this fact.

Another fact today. An American paid the huge sum of twenty six thousand pounds for three of William Blakes first editions today. They were all bound into one vol. I have never seen a first edition of William Blakes work in all my career, and to the best of my recollection I have never sold even a tenth edition of a William Blake work. I once tried to read a poem by him, but it so got me down I left the book on a park seat.

I dont suppose that American collector is darft. No one who pays 26 thousand quid for 3 books is Darft. He just happens to know what I dont know and JOLLY GOOD LUCK TO HIM. But I wish he'd paid *me* this sum. I'm blooming broke right now. Trade is awfull with me.

21st May 1958

Yesterday I had luncheon at the Hyde Park Hotel with Mr N. from Estoril in Portugal. It was a wonderfull luncheon and do you know I had for the first time ever

GULLS eggs ! They cost I think 5s. each. God ! Talk about eating money. On my oath I couldn't tell the difference between them and the eggs of Walworth at 3d. each. But my host said he liked them and they made a difference as he couldn't get 'em in Portugal.

So there I had gulls eggs and smoked salmon and all things wonderfull, *plus* lovely conversation with one of my admirers, and although it was our first meeting, in 5 minutes it was as if we had known each other 5 years. We got on well.

And do you know what he did ? Of course you dont. Well, after luncheon he took me in a taxi to Berkeley Square and from a florists named M. Stevens he bought 6 wonderful orchids in a glorious box (with gay pink ribbon) which must have cost at least a quid. And I had to take home orchids for Lizzie. She'd never *seen* an orchid in all her life. She almost cried with delight ! It gave her enormous pleasure and Mr. N. *knew it would* in advance. I was sent home in the taxi and on instruction from Mr. N. the taxi man bought one of my books out of his tip. I had to sign my book to this taxi man and I was so tight that it was a job.

Well, Diary. I put it to you. I've been ill 3 weeks. I go out. I have a *double* sherry, then again a sherry; then a white wine, then a rich red wine, then kummel – whatever that is – *plus* Gulls Eggs ! ! My God, if Mr N. had'nt sent me home in a taxi I'd *still* be in Berkeley Sq listening to the Nightingale what aint there ! All this happened yesterday but I will take days to get over it – and Lizzie has orchids ! Oh, aint it lovely to have admirers who are thoughtfull friends as well ! Yet in Walworth Ive never even had a kind word in 30 years concerning my books.

30th May 1958

I have to report that for eight days the orchids remained EXACTLY as on the day that they arrived. This, the 9th day, there is a small black mark on one petal of one orchid and a slight darkening of another orchid, and the other four are *still* as they arrived; still a JOY to Lizzie. Everyone calling has had to gaze at them, and many admitted that it was the first time they'd seen orchids close to. This is a testimonial to Moyses Stevens of Berkley Sq where the orchids were purchased that nine days later they are all practically perfect. I have no idea how long orchids are meant to last, but it will not be our fault if we dont get two weeks daily delight from them before they wilt (if that's the right word).

They lay in a fourpenny bakeing tin which we usually make a jam tart in. Its got exactly a quarter of inch of water in it and the orchids gently float on top of it. We have not changed the water, but added half a cup full every third day.

Its the first time such flowers have been in 152. But the next time I have a bit of a 'break' and make a bit of extra cash I will go me over and invest in more orchids. They give Lizzie delight and she deserves them far more than Miss Blandish ever did. I once tried to 'say it with flowers'. . . oh so long ago. A pretty lady was night after night with her husband singing a song called 'Only a rose'. She was Winnie Melville and he was Derek Oldham. She looked very much an English Rose. I saved up and I bought some yellow roses which I took to the theatre and handed in with a note of my complete admiration and my address. But what I said she obviously never heard for I didn't get an answer. I never said anything with flowers again. But someday I will – with orchids. . .

5th June 1958

Yesterday at Brighton I gave my one hundredth talk to a Rotary Club. (The first talk to Rotarians I gave was in 1941 in Camberwell. My 99th was at Chertsey a week ago.) I was keen to keep this engagement although I felt very ill and Liz had to go with me in case I got some blackouts and fell down. For five years Id tried to get a Brighton talk, but each time something prevented me. I was not going to let myself down again, so I went to Brighton. You see, diary, when I started talking at Rotary clubs a speaker with much experience of these places told me that the three toughest, hardest audiences to hold in the Rotary World were at Wakefield, Leeds and Brighton, although I forgot to ask him why. As the years have passed I managed to hold Leeds and Wakefield and I intended to see how Brighton* would accept my exclusive brand of Cockney humour.

I need not have worried. They were quite alright and gave me a fair hearing and in 25 minutes talk I was able to get NINE laughs out of them, so they were not so tough. Alas, I was only able to sell two of my books there although there were more than ninety men there and I did offer them for sale at far below cost price ! Maybe most of them are still unable to read ? I just wouldnt know. However, I sold a copy to The President of the club and to the Speakers secretary and they both promised to lend them around, so it was not quite a waste of time and genuine effort.

I recalled to Brighton Rotary how I got my first Rotarian talk. It was in 1941 and I'd made a name on the radio. There came one day to my home a big fat tough man. Would I talk at his Rotary Club ? I didnt know what Rotary was, the word meant nothing to me. He explained and then I said that I would be willing to talk for ten minutes free. He said that would not do ; it would have to be 25 minutes. And still he offered me no fee. He said he was not in the position to pay a fee so I wasnt very willing. It was war time and life was short.

Then he said that he noticed that I had two very bad

* Brighton is becoming so respectable that the pigeons now fly upside down.

teeth. He would take those two teeth out free and PAINLESS if I would talk 25 minutes. He was a dentist and would take me back to his surgery in his car immediately after the talk and in a jiffy they'd be out. He looked so strong and capable that I agreed.

Well, I gave the talk and then I went back to his place near Camberwell Green and that man gave me Bloody Hell. Never, never have I been hurt so much. He quite unnerved me for four days, and my gums were badly torn and still bleeding four days later, and took weeks to heal. When I got home I was white and shaking and bloody. I looked as if Id been in a massacre. Lizzie looked at me and then said 'My God, Freddy, what *did* them there Rotarians do to you ? They must be proper so and so's to treat you like that, and you going there FREE just to make them laugh.'

The thrill of Authorship. 1958

I learnt what little I know about the gentle art of writing by writing letters to the editor of my local newspaper. I would keep a copy of what I had written and then take notice of what they *left out* of the printed version. That was the way I learnt the economy of words and noble art of getting to the point, with the shortest number of words !

Had I had any *real* sense I would have tried to have got a job as a reporter on that paper but my freedom was extreemly precious to me. I cannot say that I even got a thrill of seeing my name or my letters in print because I always wrote very provocative and often downright rude letters on this and on that (and often on the other as well) and as that paper never paid a penny for a letter they *always* printed them – although edited nicely. It was this editing that paid *me*. After about 3 years or maybe four years of letters to the editor I felt that I'd learnt all I would ever learn and I never wrote to them again.

The first thrill Arnold Bennett got out of authorship (he said) was when they named an omelette after him at Savoy Hotel ! The first thrill that I got out of being an author was when I saw in a book trade weekly an advertisement of books urgently wanted. It was May 1934 and this was the *exact* list as printed :

W. B. Yeats	Poems . . . Cuala Press. 1913.
Walpole	Rogue Herries. Limited Ed.
V. Brittain	Testament of Youth. 1st edition.
Bason	Maugham Bibliography. Both editions.
N. Coward	Cavalcade.
Dalziell	Arabian Nights. 2 vols. 1865.

That was a thrill ! Not only was I in good company but my books were actually *wanted* in my own trade. I immediately got a copy out of my bottom drawer (and another one for luck). I got on a bus and went to the shop in Holborn where they were wanted. I showed my bibliography. Asked 7s. and they paid cash at once. They then said they'd be delighted to have another copy so out of my little attache case I brought the 2nd copy which I'd taken 'for luck' – and they paid another 7s. for it. I then revealed that I was the author of it and would be pleased to autograph them *free* ! They accepted my 'generous offer' and I got my 2nd thrill of authorship on the *same* day as I signed those 2 copies with a flourish that would not have disgraced Charles Dickens autograph. Indeed, I felt much more than Charles Dickens importance that glorious moment. After all he was *ever* so dead ! I was much alive and happy.

The Tattooed Lady. 1958

Don't stop me if you've heard this one. 'Would *you* have a Television set if your wife was tattooed ?' I know its an old one but I've a lovely reason for retelling it.

The beginning of 1958 brought me a photograph, from Birch Bay, Washington, of an extensively tattooed lady. It is up to the top of her bust and she has more tattooing on the small portion of her anatomy visible then I've ever seen on any other woman in or out of a circus.

I turned the photograph over and there on the back was written in extreemly neat handwriting

'Dear Fred, I have heard that you are a lonesome batchelor and that you like books and collect autographs. Then surely you and I should get along just perfect. For I have Gibbons Decline and Fall etc. (unabridged) tattooed on my back, Tolstoys War and Peace on my front – *and* Noël Coward has autographed me in an interesting spot ! Yours for good reading, Lydia.'

Too many comments would spoil this lovely gift from Lydia, but all I can see is 4 American flags – two each side of George Washington – some wonderfull designs and a picture which looks like a saint at the top of right arm, plus a pattern of lace work a few inches from her neck. Her very charming face is not tattooed and in her abundance of hair there is a very saucy feather.

This is indeed a feather in my cap as well. It is not every day that a 'Limey' gets a preposal from a celebrated American lady (and I am sure she's very celebrated). I am writing to Birch Bay to ask if I can read Gibbons Decline and Fall as I am on the Decline but have not yet Fallen. If she ever comes to England I will tattoo Fred Bason in another interesting spot to keep Mr Coward company !

By this very same post (no I am not kiddin in either case) came a letter from Noël Coward on Broadway saying that he will keep his word and will both edit and introduce my Fourth Diary !

This is the Red Letter climax to my humble literary career. Mr Coward is a man you cant buy or bribe. If he says 'No' then no amount of money will make him change his mind. I am glad he's said Yes and I suppose its a reward because I had my 2 bottom front teeth knocked out in an attempt to defend his reputation against a swine with an evil tongue who was twice my weight – and I *didn't* send Mr Coward the bill for 50s. which it cost me to have a plate with 2 teeth and 2 bits of 'gold' wire on them to conceal the gap.

At the time of writing Ive sent the editor of *The Saturday Book* the photo of Lydia because John Hadfield enjoys a good laugh and besides being my editor is also quite a fan of mine. Its been my rule in 30 years of factual writing to always send the evidence and proof *with* my articles. This rule always pays dividends as when some disbelieving people write to the editor saying I'm kiddin he saves me postage stamps I can ill afford by replying for me that he is satisfied with the evidence.

Its nice to know that Noël Coward had seen Lydia before me. Its rather like walking in the steps of the master ! Perhaps Mr Coward was more interested in War and Peace ? (I've not read that either.) I am pretty sure that dear Lydia didn't write to him in *quite* the same way as she did to me – if she's ever written to him at all. But if the Gods are kind and I do meet Lydia and coming from Birch Bay she gets me out of the wood of *Batchelorhoodness* (thats a lovely word) I will make jolly sure that Noël Coward is invited to the wedding if only for another view of the landscape! Me, I aint never been jealous in all my life. I like spreading pleasure and I do sincerely believe in international good will. . . hence I close this with my address 152 Westmoreland Rd London S.E. 17, 10 minutes from Big Ben in a taxi.

Come on Lydia my tattooed admirer, let me read you !

June 1958

Extract from a letter from an entirely *unknown* lady living in Kensington today, Saturday, 7th June :

'Neither I nor any of my six sisters would think of going to bed with a man *unless* we were married !'

This made my day. Work that one out for yourself. Second time you read it, it has *quite* a differant meaning.

I do get a queer mail. And from Kensington at that !

Show Business in 1958

He was a very poor old man and practically broke. He did not have the money for a desperately needed operation so he agreed to have a free operation on Television. The operation went on the screens but alas the old man died (although the viewers never knew that). The doctor felt it his personal duty to inform his patient's wife who was sitting beside the producer in the controll room. When he told the wife she just shrugged her shoulders, sighed and said, 'Oh well – that's SHOW BUSINESS !'

It happened in U.S.A. (of course) and the information came on a p.c. from an unknown admirer who felt I ought to know this true incident in modern life.

Romance in 1958

'And when he became too fresh you know what I did ? I slapped him so hard he fell out of bed !'

Reflections On Broadcasting. 1958

Without looking it up I have been broadcasting since about 1932. I have always found the B.B.C. utterly fair and square and indeed generous in their dealings with me – 75 engagements. I only found one really hopelessly hard to please producer and she in one afternoon broke my nerve and nearly made me grey with 7 cuts and 24 alterations in a 9 min talk – till it ended at 4 min 3 seconds with a script so changed that it had to go back to be retyped. And I went into the W.C. and had a good cry ! Once, only once in 75 times. I've been lucky !

I have never made a B.B.C. *friend* because I always felt it would be wrong, since they might have a script out of friendship – and that I would *never* allow. But I must record the fact that I made some friendly acquaintance-ships. These people were *most* kind to me between 1932 and 1957 : Janet Quigley, Jean Melville, Norman Collins, Joan Gilbert, Michael Bell and Mary Adams. Each of these 6 people knew what a bundle of nerves I was and made the path easier in some way or another. I owe a debt of gratitude to all six.

I cant say that I've ever enjoyed broadcasting or television work. I have always been very ill when I've arrived home from a broadcast and in bed most of the next day – utterly washed out. But always I've done my best – my *very* best – to please producer and public.

I believe it always best to memorise one's talk. *Not* to read it – just say it. I believe it best to talk to the announcer who sits opposite to you and *not* into the mike. I believe it best to have a drink of water before you start, no matter if you are not 'dry'. I believe it best *never* to argue with a producer – they get their way in the end so they might as well in the very beginning. I believe it best *never* to ask how much or to question the fee on the contract. Its absolutely FAIR at all times !

I've written these things down because today a young man asked for advice on how to broadcast and I said almost everything I've put down here today. And I've put it down (first time ever) in case I ever get asked again – which is doubtfull.

I wish I had the calmness of Cliff Michelmore !

1958

I find that when I have added up this and that and taken away those and them, I have made £82 out of the entire proceeds royalties and what not of *Diary Three*. It took me over 2 years to get together – day by day with not a let up in any day. Thats £41 a year for a *successfull* Diary, praised by 101 newspapers *and* G. Harding. Blimey, it aint even the wages of SIN !

The Live Ghost : The most inexplicable Adventure of my Life

Here and there throughout my diaries there is the letter K, standing for Kathleen. She was the joy of my twenties; with her by my side. I could have made the grade and really become someone. She was a very handsome woman and I adored her. But I found to my cost that she only took me up as a novelty, having no affection for me, or indeed for any man at all : she was frigid. Her mother was a warm, kindly woman, and knew just how I felt about Kathleen, but said she'd jilted one man right on the steps of the altar and ruined his life, and didn't want me to be hurt as well.

When this one-sided affair finally ended, I was a very sick man and weary at heart, and I was ordered away for a rest in quiet and peaceful surroundings. K's mother graciously found me a lovely picturesque spot in Hampshire and I went down there to complete a book, to get some fresh air and to forget my unhappy love affair. (Thirty years later K is still an old maid – but now has religious mania – so it was as her mum said it would be !) The place I stayed at was a huge loft, above a storage place, that had once very long ago been a water mill. It was in the tiny village of Langstone, which is near to Havant at the foot of the toll bridge over to Hayling Island.

It was a lovely little village of no more than twenty houses and just one tiny main street. Go along this road from the former mill and cross the main Havant–Hayling Road and there facing you is a lane which leads solely to marshes and smooth mud for several miles. By skirting the mud it is possible to get, via this lane, on a shorter route to Portsmouth. But it takes some doing and so is a seldom used lane.

I'd been five days at Langstone and was feeling well and quite happy, when I decided to take the short cut via the marsh land and on to the road to Portsmouth, as it was a city I longed to visit. I will stress that I was reasonably well, had slept well the night before and was forgetting the unhappiness of loving a slab of marble ! It was ten in the morning, the birds were singing and the sun was shining. It held the promise of a really lovely September day.

Suddenly in the lane I stopped. I felt so uneasy; I went cold. There, not twenty feet away from me, on the ground, lay a very old man. He was quite naked and he only had half of a right leg. There was a sort of foggy mist around him but I could see him quite clearly. This vision of an old man was tall and very thin, there was matted hair on his chest and he had a hawk-like nose (the Duke of Wellington style). I walked two or three paces forward then I stopped again. I looked around and even behind me. There was no one at all around – and there was a strange uncanny silence; there less than two minutes before, the birds had been chirping their songs, there was no song now.

I stepped forward slowly till I couldn't have been more than twelve feet from the man, when he entirely vanished. He didn't just fade away. He simply disappeared in a second and so did the mist around the figure. I felt so uneasy that I had to sit on a tree stump at the side of the road to compose myself again. I felt downright UNEASY.

When I was more myself again, I took out a note-book from a small haversack I carried on my jaunts (in which to carry home books that I bought on my travels) and then I drew a picture of the ghost's head and chest – and then added a rough drawing of the exact position I'd seen him in on the ground. I took trouble over the drawings, closing my eyes several times to get again the exact picture of the man from my mind's eye. Not that I could *ever* forget such a striking face ! Hawk-like nose, deeply sunken eyes, sunken cheeks, gaunt and clean shaven, but some grey whiskers at the end of his pointed chin. Very thin flat chest, and a great deal of long grey hair on it. Right leg was cut off just above the knee-cap and the rounded stump was sticking slightly up from the ground. I drew it all, to the best of my ability, with a thick blue pencil (the only one I had with me). Having completed the picture I then smoked a cigarette.

I reckon I was all of half an hour in that lane – then I got up and made my way through the marshland and onto the Portsmouth Road. It took about an hour more to get to Portsmouth and I stayed four hours in that city. Returning that afternoon to my Langstone digs, I wrote out the whole incident – and then entirely banished it from my mind. I didn't tell *anyone* at all about it either, there or when I returned home, in case they laughed at me.

However, in February of 1949 I happened to have the good fortune to meet in Twickenham (of all places) Walter de la Mare and felt that it might be of some slight interest to him if I told him about my one and only ghost. I knew he was interested in the uncanny and the uneasy and was a good one to tell the eerie to and get a hearing without the laughter.

He was gracious enough to say I told it all extremely well and he was himself convinced that I'd seen a ghost. And he *believed* in ghosts. He suggested that I ought to write it and suggested it was unusual enough for *The Saturday Book*. It so happened that I had some three weeks before been sending to the editor of that annual an article called "The Bason Story" which consisted of pieces and patches rather like a patch-work quilt from my life. Acting on W. de la Mare's expert advice, I wrote about one thousand words of this uncanny experience and called it 'The One-Legged Man'. Leonard Russell, the editor, said that it was splendid and just what he needed and in October 1949 the adventure appeared on Page 105 of Volume 9 of *The Saturday Book*. When the galley proofs arrived, in May, I had no changes whatsoever to make to the mss, so with Mr Russell's permission I gave it to W. de la Mare because without his suggestion I would never have written it with a view to publication. I believed my own eyes – I did not care if anyone else in the world believed it or not – but I had no wish to be laughed at, or for some reader to suggest that I was drunk at ten in the morning in a Hampshire lane, in September 1945. I was extremely sober. Not once during my stay there did I enter a public house.

My work for Volume 9 got favourable press reviews and some mail from admirers all over the world. But no one at all commented on my ghost story. That pleased me for I had *no* wish to get involved in some arguments on the unnatural !

It was a bitterly cold evening in March of 1950 that I had occasion to recall Langstone to mind again. There came to my home a Mr Edward Greer. He was about 65, stiff as a ramrod. He had closely cut, almost snow-white hair, was well dressed and groomed. He explained that he lived in Havant and was a retired civil servant. He had come up to London that day to call on me, have a nice little chat and buy a few books from me. When I asked what he wanted to chat about, he drew from his pocket a piece of folded cartridge paper and when he opened it, I saw that on the paper was drawn a rough picture of a very old man with a hawk-like nose and with one leg. It was my ghost !

I went to a tallboy in my study and after a little searching around amongst stamps, autographs and rare cards, I found my own drawing of the ghost I'd made on the spot at the actual time of seeing the vision. Side by side they looked as *twins*. It was astounding, because I'd *never* ever shown anyone (not even Lizzie) the picture I'd drawn.

Mr Greer then explained that he had seen the same ghost in the same lane just FIVE years before me ! I asked him to describe the lane and he did so. He then described the body in considerable detail – even mentioning the matted grey hair on the frail chest. He agreed with me as to the leanness of the figure. But whereas I thought the head was bald, he was sure that there had been a fringe of grey hair right at the back of the head, although the dome of the head was completely bald. I closed my eyes and visualized again the figure on the ground. I could not 'see' the fringe of hair; just the bald head, with a touch of light on it where the sun peeped through the trees and touched that head. But when we discussed the matter we came to the conclusion that whereas we had seen the *same* spook, we had probably been at slightly different angles to it and so I didn't see the fringe of hair. For the rest, we were in complete agreement.

I naturally asked the retired civil servant if by chance he had made any local enquiries about our lean man and he said that he had. The spook had unnerved him just as it had me – but he said that during his career out East he'd seen many strange things and was of an inquisitive nature and intended to get to the bottom of this uncanny experience if he could do so. He said that having seen the ghost he did not go onto the marshland (as I'd done) but had retraced his footsteps, crossed the main Havant Road and gone into the village of Langstone. Half way down the main street was a tiny pub and he went in there for half a pint of ale – and another half pint to wash it down with ! Over his two glasses, he related his experience to a couple of locals in the bar. He went to great pains to describe the spectre clearly and faithfully. Neither of the locals was able to bring to mind seeing a one-legged man around there – at least not so tall and thin or with such a noticeable nose. They were sure they'd have remembered such a man.

They were still discussing the matter when in came another local and he was asked the same question. This time, Mr Greer said, he was luckier. Yes, the local said, he really *did* recall such a man, one legged, tall and very thin. He walked with one crutch and carried over his shoulder a large sized haversack. In this haversack there were miniature Bibles and small texts and pamphlets relating to the Bible and being saved before the Day of Judgment arrives. The man was a wandering evangelist and he had the habit of buttonholing passersby and asking them rather abruptly if they had been saved ! If they said 'No' he got from his haversack a pamphlet or two and some texts and handed them over. Usually the people dropped these texts on the pavement a few yards from the cripple and he would go along after them and bend down and pick up the texts again, so as to pass onto other Sinners.

He never asked for money. He was not a beggar although he was shabbily dressed.

'I don't know how he made his living. I never saw anyone buy a Bible. He never really made a nuisance of himself.'

His approach never varied. 'Are you saved, Brother ?' 'Are you saved, Sister ?' He didn't smile. He never seemed to take offence although the locals thought he must have received some pretty rude answers in his time.

Mr Greer questioned the man as to *when* the one legged man had been actually seen in the district and he got the reply, late in 1932 and early in 1933 – then never any more. The man in the pub had seen him three or possibly four times.

'It was the size of his *nose* that brought him to my mind. As soon as you described him I knew certain sure that I'd seen such a man right here in Langstone.'

The ex-civil servant being (for a change) a *civil* civil

servant, brought all three men a pint each and there the matter ended. He was quite sure and satisfied to his own way of thinking that between 1933 and 1940 that evangelist had come to serious harm in that lane or on the marshes, and that he had seen his ghost ! He did not try any other means to trace the life of the preacher and he put the whole matter out of his mind. As far as he was concerned, it was an open and shut case until to his great astonishment, he opened Vol. 9 of *The Saturday Book* and read of my seeing the same uncanny unearthly vision in the *same* lane ! Then the whole event returned to his mind and he made it his business to come and see me.

I was downright delighted to meet him. He purchased five books from my shelves (by Baron Corvo, T.S. Eliot, L.A.G. Strong and one odd Volume of *The Saturday Book*). I think I had best put it that he saw the ghost in June 1940. I saw it in September 1945. Both of us say it was *before* noon.

I recalled the meeting with Edward Greer (with his full permission) in Volume 10 of *The Saturday Book*. I did not fear any unfavourable comments now because I had an extremely reliable witness. Just one glance at this man and you'd say he was not given to flights of fancy but, like myself, was very down-to-earth and matter of fact. Having recorded the visit I added that I would be greatly obliged and most interested if any Bible Society or mission who had ever engaged the services of a one legged evangelist would get in touch with me. I hoped this notice would catch the eye of some such organisation that distributed leaflets and religious texts especially anywhere in Hampshire, but alas no one answered my plea for information between 1950 when my appeal appeared and 1955 when there came the really sensational ending to the whole astounding event ! In the six years that had passed I'd often spoken of my ghost at lectures and talks at all manner of clubs not because I was hard up for anything to talk about, but just to see if anyone in my audiences could recall such a man. But, alas, no one ever did, although all were interested in the one legged evangelist. We now come to the sequel and the *real* reason for calling the whole thing 'The *Live* Ghost'.

It was December the first 1955. I was standing outside The Apollo Theatre in Shaftesbury Avenue, London. It was a most unpleasant night, cold and misty and bleak. I had on my best suit and my best raincoat. I'd been into the stage door and into the dressing room of Gwen Ffrangcon Davies, the well known actress. She had invited me to have tea with her, having read my first two diaries and thoroughly enjoyed them. We hadn't actually had tea (or any other drink) because she forgot to order them, so we had chatted about Ellen Terry and lots of other actresses of the past. I'd been about three-quarters of an hour with Gwen and as no tea was forthcoming, and I was to shy to ask 'Well, what about tea ?' I'd come out into the evening again.

It was about 5.50 and I was standing on the corner of Berwick Street and Shaftesbury Avenue looking in a large wine stores and deciding what luxury wine I would buy if ever my third Diary became a bestseller. Suddenly I glanced out of the corner of my eye and there on the edge of the pavement, on the extreme corner of the turning, was a one legged man. As I glanced at his hawk-like nose the hair on the back of my neck seemed to stand up and I got the biggest shock of all my life. It was the ghost come to life : *it was a live ghost*.

He was tall – an inch or two over six feet – very thin and gaunt. He wore a battered old trilby, a grubby raincoat, and there was a large haversack slung over his back. Did that haversack contain Bibles, Bible readings and texts ? I *had* to find out ! I would have given a fiver, if I'd had it, to have gone right up and asked the cripple to let me look in his haversack – but he looked a pretty tough, ugly customer and I know that would be the wrong approach. He would probably have given me a rap with his crutch for my audacity. It had to be done in a nicer way but it had to be done *somehow*. I had to talk to that man and yet I was too scared to do so. After all, I put it to you. Would you really go up to a strange man under such particular circumstances ? I had seen him lying dead in a lane in Hampshire ! He was a *live* ghost !

I walked up to him and politely touched my cap. 'Please excuse me sir,' I said. 'Don't think me either rude or mad, but I'm looking at you and seeing a living ghost !' He turned and exactly faced me and there was surprise in his sunken eyes. And he sniffed – or probably he snorted through that Duke of Wellington nose ! He didn't tell me to go to Hell or ask me if I was drunk, or just plain ignore me as one of the odd freaks of Soho. He stared at me a few seconds and then said one word : 'Explain.'

I felt that the first thing was to get to know the man and so I asked him if he would kindly give me his name and address. He refused with a one-word answer – 'No !' I then asked if he would care to step away from the corner and come under the shelter of the canopy by the gallery entrance to the Apollo Theatre, for there was now a drizzle in the air besides which we were rather in the way on that busy corner. He agreed to do that and followed me the few steps. When we got there I offered him a cigarette which he took without a thank you and a light which he did not acknowledge. Ghosts Smoked ! I was too excited to smoke. I right there and then told him as quickly as possible all that I've written here including Mr Greer's exploits. He did not interrupt and he certainly seemed interested in my narrative.

When I had finished, he said 'Well ?' I found this disconcerting. 'Well' was hardly the word I would have used if the tables had been turned – but I wasn't going to be put off.

'Well,' I said, 'it was *you* – *you*, sir, I saw in that lane. You are exactly and absolutely the *same* ! Please do answer a few questions.'

He said 'Well ?' again, which I took to be 'Yes' and so I asked if he was over seventy. He said that he was sixty-seven.

'Have you *ever* been to Langstone – it's in Hampshire ? Have you ever been travelling round Hants – if not actually in this little village ?'

He seemed to give this matter serious thought and then said he'd never been to Langstone or Hayling Island. He had perhaps been at some odd time in or around the borders of Hampshire, but not for twenty or more years, and then to the best of his recollection, *never* on foot and most certainly *never* asking people if they were saved. He laughed here, as if that struck him as extremely funny. He did look really weather beaten as if he'd been a great deal in the open air. I was in no position to question his statements. I was indeed downright grateful for his answers, and I didn't want to upset him in any way. If I handled him the right way, I had a 'scoop' for my new diary which would set the whole world talking. Although I've interviewed more than five thousand people in my journalistic career, this man was my most difficult case as yet. I felt at any moment as if he'd either fly off the deep end or vanish – and I would never be able to join together the loose threads woven by Greer and then by me so long ago ! I felt it time to get down to bare facts.

'Have you got a great deal of hair on your chest ?' I asked him.

'Do you want me to strip *here* ?' he answered.

'No sir, of course I don't. I have no wish to be personal or rude. I am just keenly interested in you. This is the strangest meeting of my life. The whole thing is weird. Just as if time has jumped *forward* and two of us have seen you in the future.'

'That's a *nice* thing to say, young man. The future ! Naked in a lonely lane !'

'No – it isn't nice but I can't see any *other* explanation to the mystery. Can you, by chance recall where you were ten years ago ? Or better still, in say June of 1940 ? Can you think back that far ? My reason for asking is because the other man saw your vision at that time. I *know* it's not easy to go back all that time – but please try !'

He did try. I could see that he was thinking and he counted off years and muttered places to himself. Time seemed to stand still. I dared not interrupt his flow of thought. For two minutes he was muttering away. I hoped that he would say 'Oh, somewhere in Hampshire.' When about three minutes had passed, I thought I'd take a big gamble and encourage him to talk so I said, 'Excuse me, sir, I don't want to take up your time for nothing, for time is valuable. Look – here is 7s. 6d. It's all I can spare at the moment. Will you please accept it and go on talking to me ?' There was a sullen, angry look in his eyes. He pushed back my hand which held the three half-crowns.

'Don't want to be *paid* to talk ! *Like* company. Interested. Put money away !'

So I put it away and waited. At last he seemed to arrive at some dates and places.

'1940. Yes, 1940. I was in Iceland. June, July 1940 I was in Iceland – or just coming away from there – could have been on the sea – or maybe Shetlands. But most of 1940 I was IN Iceland. I was there again in 1945 – that's sure. Wasn't in England. That's *sure*. Not Hampshire, *positive*.'

I asked him what he was doing in Iceland of all places, but he refused to say, telling me it was beside the point. I pointed out that a one legged evangelist had been seen in Langstone in 1932.

'Nothing to do with *me*,' said the live ghost. 'Been many things but never *that* !'

'Perhaps you have a twin brother or a relation who looks exactly like you ?'

'Could *anyone* be just like me ?' He looked at his half leg and sniffed. 'No, I've never had a brother and I've no relations at all. Alone in the world.'

I told him that I was in the exact same boat and had no relations either. He seemed from that moment to thaw and unbend. I gave him another cigarette and this time he actually said thank you. And when I gave him a light he said 'Much obliged.' It was at this moment that I asked his name again and he told me to call him Pat. (But he did *not* have an Irish accent.)

I would guess that we had stood fifteen minutes under the gallery shelter of the Apollo Theatre, and I was getting cold, although I had on a good deal thicker coat than Pat had.

I felt it time to make some sort of move but I was extremely reluctant to let Pat go, in case I never met him again. He looked very thin and I was sure a good meal would do him a world of good. What I really wanted to do was to show him the drawings of the ghost I had at home. He would then see and realise that it was all really something and not a figment of imagination. If he put my drawing and his face to a mirror, he would see they were one and the same. If I could convince him, then I could perhaps *save his life* ! It was, to my way of thinking, sure that this man would end up stark naked and stiff – very dead – in Langstone Lane and I felt if I could prove to the hilt by the drawings, then he would be convinced and never visit Hampshire all the rest of his life, and so would prolong it by avoiding the place of tragedy.

'Well, Pat, will you have a meal with me in Lyons ? It's only in Coventry Street. We could have a snack and hot coffee. My treat. Let's spend the rest of my bit of money. Its just enough for a small snack each. Do come along sir.'

'Not dressed well enough,' he said, looking at his dirty raincoat.

'Heck ! If Lyons don't mind, I don't mind – why should you mind ? Clothes mean nothing these days. I'd be happy to have your company.'

'Skip it ! I said I'm not dressed up enough. Leave it at that.'

'Well, will you kindly come home with me ? It's on the number twelve bus route from Piccadilly and where I live is Walworth, and that's a slum district and your clothes will be entirely unnoticed down my way. I've a very kind housekeeper and she will give you a good meal - the best she can dish up – I promise you. I want to show you the sketches Mr Greer and I made and they are at home. I think – indeed I'm blooming sure – you'll agree that although they are only rough sketches, they are the dead image of you.'

'The *dead* image,' he said. 'The dead image.' He seemed to like the sound of that phrase and as he said it his false teeth clicked over the words. He quite ignored my hospitality and I didn't like to repeat the offer. Then I recalled to mind the drawings and had a brainwave.

I said to Pat, 'I'll bet you one shilling that if you take off your hat the dome of your head is entirely bald and you only have a little fringe at the back – sort of like a monk. No hair except right at the back.'

He shrugged his shoulders and laughed, then he took off his battered and dirty old trilby. I was right ! Just as I'd described, so it was. And I'd been positive I'd be right. By some astounding flash forward in time I was seeing my ghost absolutely alive. It was amazing and quite unaccountable but it was true. I would have bet fifty pounds at that moment he had long grey hairs on his chest – just as Greer and I had seen.

'What's all this leading up to, young man ?' he asked. 'It's intriguing – nice word that – intriguing. But we must arrive at a solution. There must be a summing up.'

'But you can't sum this up, sir. This is the future skipped into the past. I know it sounded very fantastic, but all I've said is the naked truth. One thing is certain sure. You must give Hampshire a wide berth from now onwards.'

'Heavens ! Why ?'

'Why, ain't it obvious ? You will die there ! Alone – naked – stiff and starving. I say starving because we saw your body, so flat and thin.'

'A man's got to die *somewhere* !'

'I agree with that, but dash it all, you don't *have* to run into trouble, sir. It comes to all of us soon enough, without walking towards it !'

He didn't reply. At this point, he put his hand into the pocket of his raincoat and took out the largest watch I've ever seen in all my life. It was bigger than even a large size railway watch. It was more like a travelling clock without its leather case, and he carried it loose in his pocket. It looked very odd – but somehow in keeping with my live ghost. He glanced at it and then casually put it back in his raincoat. Then he pulled his large haversack from his side to the front of him. He didn't open the haversack, he didn't touch the buckle. He just thrust his thin hand into a corner of it and got out a small deep brown bottle. He unscrewed the bottle's top and took two quite large size pills from it which he swallowed at once, without any trouble. His prominent adams apple just pulled up his very thin neck once and then went down – like a plug in the sink. Oh, I did admire him for this feat ! Never in all my life have I been able to swallow a pill without the aid of water to wash it down with. Pat's pills were *really* big ones. I stared at him. He returned to his cut-rate conversation by saying one word. 'Heart !' I assumed that he meant that he had a bad heart and the two pills eased the trouble. He shrugged his shoulders.

'What the hell ! Not a fit man in any twelve you care to pick out over sixty today. Not one. Well – must go. Things to do. Any more questions ?'

I could easily have asked a dozen. The main one was *what* did he carry in that haversack – besides that little bottle ? I asked him right there and then what did it contain ?

'None of your business, sonny. Keep your nose clean.'

I offered him the 7s. 6d. to let me peep inside. He laughed.

'If you made it seven pounds six, it would *still* be no.'

I didn't press the matter. I asked his business and his answer was 'Bits and pieces. Fiddling. A little pension. . . just enough. No ties. Free !'

I said that I understood, but blimey – I didn't ! Then he said that he'd better go. All been interesting. . . Mr. . . I don't have your *name*. I told it to him but it didn't ring a bell. (I didn't really think it would. He didn't look the sort of man who would read anything but a newspaper and only that if he found one on his journeys.)

Then he said something I'd only heard once before in my life and that only in an American film about Virginia, some fifteen or twenty years ago. He said, 'It has *pleasured me* to meet you, Mr Bason. Interesting meeting. . . and hearing about my ghost. Be a topic. Yes, it's *pleasured* me.' He held out his thin hand with long sharp fingernails. His hand was very cold. I drew mine away quickly. Shaking hands with him was *not* pleasant. He had been leaning against the wall for most of our conversation. Now he drew his crutch towards him and then under his arm. Half his trouser leg was folded over and attached to the top half with a large safety pin. He nodded when I said 'Goodbye and good luck' and then he hobbled away up Berwick Street – just six or seven paces. Then he turned and said out loud : 'Well – *are you saved ?*'

My blood ran cold. I didn't attempt to answer him and

with a laugh he turned away and the misty night swallowed him up. I walked into Piccadilly and got my bus to Walworth. Thinking it all over on the bus as I recorded the event in my note book, I was in the end rather glad he had not accepted my invitation to come home with me. There was really something odd about Pat and I've an idea my dear housekeeper would have been scared of him. Truth to tell, I was afraid of Pat and yet I could not, for the life of me, say why. He had treated me most civilly and answered most of my questions. He had refused my money offer . . . and yet . . .

The whole meeting with Pat I recalled in Volume 16 of *The Saturday Book*, which was published in October 1956, because I was so sure its readers would be interested in the meeting. Bai jove – they were !

I *did* meet Pat again – just once. It was in February 1957. I had been in Charing Cross Road and I cut through one of the alleys on my way to my publishers in Soho Square. It was just about three o'clock in the afternoon. I saw him sitting on a step in Greek Street, close to a public house. I crossed the road and said 'Hello, Pat, my ghost.' He looked up at me with glazed eyes. He was dead drunk ! I passed on. I have never seen him again although I've searched many times in the past year. I wonder where he is ? Is he now a *real* ghost ?

P.S. : Mrs. E. Bird of Oxford saw my ghost in the same lane in 1939. She's just told me about him.

Night with a starlet. 1959

In November 1958 I wrote a letter to the *Star* newspaper, telling them that although I was a rather famous Cockney author, known to far over 12,000,000 people all round the world, no one had ever invited me to a film premire. I had stood for years beside big policemen watching handsome men escort beautifull stars to shows, but never had I been invited, nor for that matter had I a pretty lady to take. Low and behold the day after the publication of my letter the publicity manager of Associated British Pathé Limited wrote saying that he could and *would* provide me with a Rolls Royce car, a very pretty actress, front row seats for the film premire of *Girls at Sea* at the Empire Theatre, and a nice supper for both of us after the show at Kettners. Would I like to go ? WOULD I ? Cor luv a blooming duck. I accepted at once (in case they changed their minds) and so on November 20th I escorted Dorinda Stevens, a very very pretty actress, to this class DO, and a very nice time was had by all. One of the STAR nights of my life. I will never forget it.

I had my photo taken several times with Dorinda. We saw this comedy film in great comfort. Then we had a very very lovely and expensive supper at Kettners.

Now at long last I know what it is like to escort a pretty starlet to a premire. Mark you, diary, I was myself rather 'all at sea', in keeping with the title of the film, but it was all very enjoyable

P.S. Changing from winter clothes into evening dress for this memorable occasion, I caught an unearthly chill that turned to flu and I was very ill for eleven days after that night out. But it was worth it. For just ONCE in my life I was made to feel that I was really SOMEONE. Just for one glorious night !

I go fishing. 1959

Early this summer an unknown lady came to my home and asked to buy copies of my first three diaries, but said they had to be cheap because they were for a Pole with *one* leg ! This gave me such a good laugh that I deducted 2/6 and she seemed pleased with the deal. I then forgot all about it until late September when the actual Pole (still with one leg) wrote me saying how very much he had enjoyed my recollections, *but* that they lacked *one* thing –

Fishing ! There was nothing whatever about angling in them and this was his one disappointment as he was a keen angler. I felt bound to tell him that I had never handled a rod or been fishing in all my life – and that I only wrote true adventures. I also said that although I longed to be known as the modern Samuel Pepys, I had no intention of copying Isaac Walton and that Isaac could rest peacefully in his grave and I would never disturb him because fishing in sea or stream had no appeal to me.

As far as I was concerned that closed the matter – I'd had my say and the Pole had a holograph letter to put into one of my Books ! I was surprised (and delighted) when a week later the Pole wrote saying that I didn't realise what I was missing and as a reward for the laughter my books had given him, he would allow me to be his guest and he would pay all expenses for a day's fishing at Henley-on-Thames, his favourite fishing haunt. He named a day and suggested that I came the night before and stayed with him and his wife that night so that we made an early start the next morning.

Looking at my engagement book I found that I had no talks to give and was free to accept his graciously offered hospitality and having nothing whatever to lose and something in the form of a brand new experience to gain, I gratefully accepted. His home was but 100 yards from Bethnal Green Public Library which is an hour's journey from my home in Walworth. I arrived there promptly at seven and was given by the Pole and his wife a nice welcome and a hearty dinner.

Stas, the Polish gentleman, is also a keen book man and we talked books and writing till around ten. I got my first shock when I found out that we had to be up at FIVE in order to catch the 5.30 from Liverpool Street to somewhere down the line, where we would then catch a local train which would land us at Henley some time later, all things being equal (which they seldom are !). With the prospect of up at FIVE (first time in 10 years I've been up so early) I was very willing for early to bed – and so we all slept – in different beds.

Stas woke me at 4.45 with very hot tea. I washed as he prepared the breakfast (his wife was wise enough to continue her beauty sleep). We then had breakfast. A liberal amount of sandwiches had been cut and packed up the previous night for our expedition. All that we needed were flasks of coffee and these Stas prepared with an expert hand. We left Bethnal Green at just after five and made our way to the Underground station where we probably got the first train to Liverpool Street. I don't recall a thing about this section of the journey as I was still almost asleep ! I know that Stas carried tackle and gear and food etc. weighing all of 60 pounds, and I carried about 12 to 15 lbs. of additional gear, the flasks and oddments including a hangover ! Poor Stas with an artificial leg was, of course, a very slow walker and found stairs extremely tiresome. I am usually a fast walker (there is only 8 stone of me, whereas there was 14 stone of Pole !) and time and again I found myself walking 3 times as fast as him and pulling myself up quickly in order for him to catch me up. It was most thoughtless of me – but I *couldn't* break a lifetime habit of quick little steps instead of very slow long ones in one early morning.

Liverpool Street Station seemed deserted. Our train could have held 400 but there was not 20 on it and we had a compartment to ourselves, and by the time we had put down all our many parcels, packages and haversacks, plus a multitude of rods, we *needed* the whole compartment ! Stas read a newspaper. I tried to read – but fell asleep !

About an hour later we had to change trains. It took us all of 5 minutes to gather our goods and chattels together to get *out* of one train, and there 4 platforms away stood the train which would land us in Henley . . . and a very bright porter in the keen morning air brightly told us we had 3 minutes in which to catch it – or wait an hour for the next ! He didn't offer to help us. Our clothes (and Stas had particularly asked me to come in my *oldest* clothes) probably told him we were not good for much of a tip. This is where my fast little legs came into real service. I picked up my 12 pounds of this and that, and dashed up the stairs, along a bridge, and over 4 lines of tracks, down the stairs and ran like the wind to the local train's guard. Rather breathlessly I told him my pal had ONE leg and was a Pole *at that* (I don't know why I added this information) and *please* could he wait a minute or two more as my pal found the stairs difficult to negotiate. He was a kind-hearted guard and told me not to worry – he'd wait. I then rushed back up the stairs, met Stas half-way, took the huge collection of rods and parcels of food and rushed back to show the guard we were *still* coming and would be there soon – all things being equal. That train went out 4 minutes late, but the passengers didn't seem to notice or protest at the delay ! (Stas had been there many times before so they probably all knew about his lameness !). We slung everything down just inside the carriage as it was no time to mess about putting things tidy-like. The journey into Henley was restful, and I *needed* the rest ! Stas was cool, calm and extremely collected. Nothing put him out. I've never come upon a more good tempered early morning companion. I fear that I wasn't good company, and as I had nothing to say, I said nothing. I just looked out of the window at the rain. Oh ! I have forgotten to tell you about the rain ? It was raining very hard when we left Bethnal Green and it was raining harder still when we reached Henley-on-Thames. I would not have been a tiny bit surprised if anyone had said the Thames was overflowing and that Henley was flooded – that's how badly it was raining.

Now, although we had been undercover most of the way, my clothes were very damp and sticky and my old boots were leaking and my socks were damp ! A *fine* start to a days fishing. I didn't even feel a bit happy. Indeed, I felt browned off and we hadn't even started ! There we were in Henley Station and I had no idea at all how far we were to where the fishes hung out in their haunts, but was sure it *wasn't* in the High Street. Thinking we then faced a long tough wet walk, I had some of my coffee (we each had our own flasks) and pulled myself together. Stas must have noticed the expression on my face – and he called a taxi ! Well, blow me down, this was doing things in style ! I became more cheerful. The taxi driver knew *exactly* the part of the river where my host wanted to go and he also helped us with our kit. We were by the side of the Thames 15 minutes later. (It would have taken all of an hour to have walked at a Stas's pace.) He made arrangements for the same taxi to pick us up at 3.30. That was a load off my mind because after 5 or 6 hours fishing, I didn't want to face an hours walk back to the station loaded down not only with gear but FISH as well ! From where we left the taxi to where we actually settled down to fish was all of an half a mile and probably more. To me all the river looked alike and I couldn't think why we had to go over field and path to get to the *exact* haunt, and I didn't care to ask why – if you ask a silly question you are entitled to a silly answer !

There we were about a quarter of a mile or so from Henley Lock on the left hand side of the Thames, with the rain coming down and the river flowing fast and furious. Everything had to be unpacked. The first job was to put a pole into a pole, and then an umbrella on top of the pole ! Then you pushed the other end into the ground and the huge umbrella stood up. Although there was a sharp steel point at the end of the pole, the fury of the wind and rain would not allow this umbrella to stand up so we could shelter beneath it. We spent a quarter of an hour in the rain pushing that pole into the flint-like pathway close to the side of the Thames and then gave it up and compromised with one edge of the large umbrella touching the ground and us two cramped together underneath it sorting out the gear, and fixing up the rods and fish's food.

Half an hour went by before Stas was satisfied with the rods (they cost £60) and I got my first shock as I saw the large tin of maggots. My goodness I'd *never* seen so many horrible little maggots before ! And we had large parcels of soft soaked bread that looked an unwholesome mess as well. Stas looked at the rain and at the river and said it was *a lovely day for fishing* ! Just the weather for making the fish bite. They came up more frequently in the rain (what, to get wet – wasn't they wet enough ? asked me). Having got out a couple of portable chairs we were ready – and I was soaked and cold. I was then given my first lesson in how to put maggots on the hook – and how the poor little things wriggled about. Next came the lesson of casting the rod and this took me a long time to learn. Obviously there was a knack in it, and very obviously I hadn't got the knack. My line was either too short to cast far in, or I gave out too much line and it caught on the grass and bushes en route to river. I got, at times, in a hopeless tangle. I must have tried 20 times before the maggot went with the line some 5 feet or less from the bank. Stas on the other hand, cast his out some 8 feet the very first time and then rigged up some device whereby he put his rod into a V-shaped rest with a bell on it and all he had to do then was meditate and listen for the bell which told him a fish was biting. Easy – ain't it ! Ain't science wonderful ! And there's me with a less impressive and smaller rod trying to cast it to Stas's instructions . . . and getting more browned off and more wet – because it was *not* possible to stay under the umbrella *and* push out a line. You could go under the umbrella *after* the line was in the river and the fisherman's rest was pitched into the ground and the bell was attached to rod and rest. My line was thirty minutes late getting all settled and my friend had two bites (what got away) during the time. Talk about bolting the stable after the horse had gone. I was absolutely soaked by the time I crawled *underneath* the umbrella ! I then had coffee which I badly needed because my hands were frozen ! So this was Fishing ! My goodness, and they call it SPORT !

From time to time during the next two hours I got off that tiny stool either because I was stiff, or because my bottom was sore from that hard wooden stool, or because the bell rang, or because the coffee went through me and I had to run to a distant bush ! I *never* had a bite. I *never* caught a fish. I nearly caught my death of cold. Stas had caught five small fishes – well, he called them small, they looked 4 to 6 inches long to me. He did tell me what species they were but I soon forgot the details, as fish is all fish to me. He put the fish in a net basket that hung into the river on a pole, just beside his line. He was undoubtedly happy and quite at peace with the world. As far as he was concerned there was *not* a cloud in the sky. But me, I was most horribly wet and cold. Not a cloud in the sky ! Golly, let me assure you that the sky was *all* cloud, dark, gloomy, low hanging, heavy clouds, and it *still* rained. We broke off fishing at about 12.30 for food and drink and I found to my horror that I had drunk *all* my hot coffee ! ! I had to have some of my host's coffee in order to get the sandwiches down. By the time I'd had 3 sandwiches I also had acute indigestion ! His wife had used new white bread – and I usually have 2 days old brown bread. Had I known his number I'd have phoned up Gilbert Harding for some of his indigestion tablets ! We were alone. The nearest fisherman to us was 200 yards away. The traffic on the river was light – only mugs would have gone *on* the river on that day, just as to my mind only *mugs* were sitting on little stools cramped up together under an umbrella watching a couple of lines and listening for a couple of bells to ring by the river !

By about one thirty I had had just about ENOUGH. There is a limit to everything and I had reached the limit for the time being. After all, the taxi was not calling to pick us up until 3.30. Without a change of scenery and some really hot tea and a hot meal I could go on no longer with this sport called Fishing. Maybe I hadn't meditated. I'd been told angling time was the time for thinking. If I had spoken *my* thoughts aloud, Stas might have been vastly annoyed ! After all he had paid all expenses for a happy day out for us. It wasn't his fault that it was raining or that my boots leaked or that the legs of my trousers were soaked or that I had indigestion, or that I was stiff, sore and cold. If all things had been equal, one could not have wished for a more pleasant companion. But I just didn't feel like discussing the merits of Rupert Brooke's poems, Paderwski's piano playing, or what should be and shouldn't be in diaries. Every time the little bell rang on the end of my line I'd make a dash out to welcome the little fish, but they were mighty cute fishes at Henley and didn't want a welcome from a raw beginner ! I'd done all I could and now I had to get away or I'd collapse from the cold or get pneumonia from my wet clothes. I suggested we break off our fishing and go for a nice brisk walk and find a hot meal, but right at that moment my Polish pal was playing a very large frisky fish and said 'You go old man. I'm quite happy here.' And he really was happy. Me. I was feeling miserable !

Well, I walked a quarter mile to the Lock and as far as I can recall this was the nearest I'd been to lock gates in years, but I passed over a narrow wooden bridge without looking at the scenery, as a tiny cottage had a large notice saying TEAS. Inside the cottage I knocked, banged and called out for a whole 5 minutes before a middle-aged lady came from a back room to attend to me. Yes, I could have a pot of really *hot* tea for ninepence. Another five minutes went by before the pot, sugar, milk and small cup arrived. An experienced eye told me that I could get three good cups of tea out of that sized pot and I paid the ninepence willingly. I then took the tray into the diningroom – where no one dined, as they didn't serve meals ! Fortunately there were no other customers. I put my soaked cap over the teapot. I thought it might dry out a bit, and in any case would serve as a tea-cosy till the tea 'drawed'. There was no fire – the room was damp and chilly. I took off my raincoat and slung it over a chair. Then I searched my pockets for paper. I found a catalogue for Hutchinson's Books, a couple of the special order forms Hutchinson's kindly print for me regarding the 'Saturday Book', a leaflet from the Abbey Building Society, a letter from an admirer and an unkind letter from a writer which was full of jealousy.

With these various papers in front of me I made socks for my leaking boots. The Building Society's leaflet was on art paper and the strongest, and this torn to something like the shape of a couple of feet, made the foundation, and Hutchinson's catalogue made five thin layers above it. I had neither knife or scissors and had to tear it all neatly with my frozen fingers. I then took off my very wet socks and tried to dry my feet on the letters. I put the Saturday Book order forms inside my socks and then put back my socks. It took some time to get the rucks out of the paper which had occurred as I replaced my socks. The dry paper was a little more comfortable.

I was stuffing the improvised socks into my boots, when a couple of working class men came into the room and one of them brilliantly observed to me that it was a nasty day. I had to agree. The other then asked if my boots were leaking, and I just nodded as I continued the tricky job of putting the paper flat. Having at last got it to lay level, I then had the devil's own task to put my damp sock encasing a still damp foot into that boot with the paper remaining flat. It just wouldn't work. The thickness of the sheets of paper left no room for my foot to go in. Reluctantly, I had to take my foot out again and throw away some of the paper. I finally settled for 2 thicknesses of the Building Society art paper and got one foot settled in nicely on that.

All this time the other foot was getting more and more frozen, so I used all the surplus paper to rub away at the sock and foot – and the two men gazed at me with great interest. The cover of the Hutchinson's catalogue was craft paper and reasonably stout in texture, and three layers of it went into my other boot. Again the great trouble of getting it to lay down as my damp sock went into the boot. Three times I had to take it out and start all over again – and all this time my tea in the pot was 'drawing' (it could have drawn a van to Henley and back by this time !).

All this time the two men ate sandwiches from bags and drank their tea and gazed at me. I felt like passing my cap over to them for a contribution for I am so sure I was entertaining them with my antics ! I would say at a rough guess it took me twenty minutes to do the paper-into-boots-job. Of course they'd leak again the moment I got out into the wet but for the time being they did feel like feet and not dead damp meat. I took my hat off the teapot and made myself a cup of tea – but alas it was no longer HOT. (Well, what did I expect !). Still it was wet and warm and I had three cups of it. I then went through my raincoat pockets and found there two post-cards of myself advertising 'Swallow Raincoats' as never getting the bird ! (Blimey, I'd given fishing the 'Bird' by now !) and stuffed both of these inside my cap because that was still wet inside – almost as wet as it was outside. With a dry pocket handkerchief I attempted to wipe my very grubby face. I found that the bottom of both trouser legs were soaked, so I turned the turnups up twice (I don't know why I did this !). On went my Swallow, which fortunately had lived up to its reputation, for after five hours of rain it had still *not* penetrated inside – my jacket was still dry ! On went the cap. I picked up the tea tray and I went with a cheerful word to the men 'I am Fred Bason and I've had a Basonful of Henley weather and b——— fishing !' Putting down the tray on the counter I departed.

It was now a fine drizzle and a cold wind. I watched two small boats pass through the lock, as I was in no real hurry to get back to the battle of the little fishes. After a quarter of an hour I felt I had to return in case dear Stas thought I'd drowned my little self in a fit of depression.

Crossing the wooden bridge again I walked by the side of the river. I passed a fisherman on his stool and said 'Any luck ?' 'Luck,' he said, 'Luck in *this* bleeding weather. I'm daft to be here with *my* chest ! ! !' I agreed with him. Then I saw a couple of school boys just as daft, with what looked to me like broom handles for rods with three or four feet of string and a bent pin. But by their side were two fishes quite 12 inches long ! The largest fishes I'd seen that eventful day.

Eventually I got back to my Polish friend and he welcomed me with 'Feel better now, old man ?' I said I felt fit enough to try again. In for a penny, in for a pound, and there was still about one and a half hours of fishing to do before our taxi would arrive and take us to dryness. I tried and I tried – but never a fish came my way. Stas allowed me to try his line when his bell rang, but even then they got away ! The next hour went by slowly. I looked into the net basket and found that Stas had collected 6 small fishes of assorted colours. I felt sorry for the fishes – they had done no one any harm and they certainly hadn't invited us to Henley !

At around three o'clock we prepared to depart, and the rain stopped – yes, it actually stopped ! It had rained heavily for *eight hours* ! It took us all of half an hour to get our equipment together. There was a place for everything and everything had to go into the place or it was not fixed in ! It was a lesson in neat packing to watch Stas pack the things away. His huge knapsack had a multitude of pockets and there was something for every pocket. *As we took down the umbrella the* SUN SHONE ! The first sun of the day ! It was not easy to fold up the wet huge Bookmakers size umbrella but eventually Stas was satisfied it was as neat as circumstances permitted. He was a soul of neatness. When all was packed we collected our parcels, packages, and kit and were preparing to leave when he said I'd left the paper, in which my sandwiches had been packed on the grass, and back he went and collected every scrap of paper, leaving the haunt *exactly* as he'd found it ! As we were only minus the coffee and the sandwiches and had collected much wetness, everything weighed just as heavy.

It was 3.45 when we reached the place where the taxi ought to have been waiting. It wasn't there ! I got into a bit of a stew, but my pal told me to calm down, the taxi would arrive, we had just got to be a little patient. We sat on a low wall surrounding a rich man's house and we waited . . . and the sun shone brightly. You could almost see the steam coming off our clothes. As we sat there I thought over the most astounding of all things that had happened that day. The last thing Stas had done was to throw *all* the fish *back* into the river ! We hadn't even got a single fish ! We had no proof that we had even been fishing ! It seemed to me proper potty to go fishing and *not* to *take home fish* ! He tried to explain that the pleasure was in the actual sport of fishing and that if everyone took home their catches, there'd very soon be no fish in that part of the river. I couldn't see it that way at all (and I still cannot – but then I'm no angler, as you very well know by now !). The taxi arrived at four and the extremely amiable taxi man asked if we had a good day's sport. It seems you *don't* say 'Have you caught any fish ?' You just say – 'Did you have a good day's sport ?' When I go to my sport, which is dog racing, my taxi man asks if I've backed any winners and I say 'No' when I have had a nice lot of winnings and 'Yes' on the very few times (fortunately) when I've lost ! (You can work out *why* I say this !).

On the way back to the town of Henley, Stas stopped the taxi at a small stationery-confectionary-cum-post office, where he purchased some views of the neighbourhood. I didn't want any. When we reached the railway station, we found we had 45 minutes to wait till our train went out ! Stas was contented to write letters on his postcards. I went for a walk round town. Turning to the left I found an arcade and in the bright sunshine I sauntered along looking like a tramp and feeling like one. There was one shop with 2 trays of books outside and very naturally I looked at them. The books were marked all 6d. each. I purchased 'The House of Defence' a novel by E. F. Benson, 'The Bay' by L. A. G. Strong, a Bradshaw Railway Guide for 1891 in choice condition, a magazine with an article by myself in it on Boxing recollections which I had written in 1931, and a book on old china and glass with attractive plates in it. The proprietor came out of his shop and stood by my side the whole time I was choosing these books. I am very sure he thought I was there to steal them !

I gave him 2/6 for the lot, and looking at me he gave me 6d. back and said he was quite satisfied with 2/- ! That was very nice of him and cheered me up no end. At my request he found some string and made a small parcel with a handle on it. (Naturally, he didn't know that at the station was my share of the load of gear to be carried back to Bethnal Green.) On arrival at the station I found that my companion had written all his letters, and I minded our gear whilst he found a pillar box. He particularly wanted them to be post-marked Henley. At least he could prove he'd been there – but I couldn't and I didn't want to do so either. If I never saw Henley-on-Thames again it would suit me alright.

We arrived back at Stas's flat about just after 7.30. Naturally his wife, Iris, wanted to know what I'd thought about my first days fishing, and naturally I wanted to think out a *civil* answer. Stas came to my rescue by explaining it had rained eight hours and I'd had no luck with my line. These two statements seemed to cover the whole matter and I just nodded in complete agreement. I had a loan of the bathroom for ten minutes or so, and devoted five of it to taking out all the paper from my boots and my socks. The whole lot was a sodden mess I then replaced it with toilet paper and put the wet paper down the lavatory. The next five minutes was devoted to making myself look a little more presentable.

Stas washed whilst I steamed before a nice fire. Then we had a hearty meal, and I found that I was enormously hungry. The table was bare when we had tucked in. I returned to the fireside and then realised I *had* to pull myself together and quick, or I'd go fast asleep. I shook myself and getting my clothes I made my farewells. Thanking Stas for a memorable day, I assured him that it would live in my memory and my diary for the rest of my life. When he suggested we had another day of it I did *not* take him up. I'd had enough for a lifetime !

It was just after ten when I reached home and there was Lizzie waiting to welcome me with a big fire, a singing kettle, and on the table was a large plate of potatoes cut up neatly into chips ready for frying. All that I had in my hand was 5 books tied up with string.

'Where's the fish ?' she said.

'There ain't any fish !'

'What – no fish and you been all day fishing. What happened ?'

'The man threw them back into the Thames.'

'The man threw them back ?'

'The man threw them back !'

'What ! Was they bad ?'

'How could they have been bad when they'd just been caught.'

'I mean wasn't they eatable ones ?'

'How the heck do I know. I know nothing but that they looked a bit small.'

'How many was there ?'

'Oh ! Seven or eight.'

'And he threw back seven or eight fishes. But Fred, sardines are small, and you are lucky to get seven in one tin !'

'Oh ! They were bigger than sardines. They must have been six inches long and rather fat. Only he said they were small and that in any case he only went fishing for the sport of it, and *not* to catch and keep fish !'

'Is he all there ?'

'Yes, I think so. Mark you, he *is* a Pole.'

'Oh ! He's a Pole.' There was a long silence then. After a while she said – 'Isn't there a fish called a Perch ?'

'Yes, I'm sure there is a fish called that.'

'Then he *should* be a fisherman. Rod, Pole and Perch. I'm *sure* I've heard of that expression somewhere.' I nodded. I'd heard of it as well, although I was too sleepy to sort out its meaning.

'What about these here chips ?' asked Lizzie.

'Well what about them !'

'I got 'em all ready so that when you brought the fish home we would have a lovely fish and chips supper. I know how you like that.'

'I've seen enough fish for today ! Throw the chips away. I ain't hungry !'

'Throw nothing away ! They will do for dinner to-morrow. I will go up the road tomorrow morning and get a couple of pieces of skate for a shilling, and we'll have a nice dinner. You know I don't allow waste.'

'Can I have a bowl of hot water ? I reckon I'm going to have one heck of a cold. It rained eight hours, and I'm still wet from head to foot.' (It started to rain again as I left Bethnal Green, and it had rained all the way home).

'It don't sound as if you had a *really* pleasant day' said Lizzie.

'That, my dear, is an *under*statement !'

As she was getting the footbath, she asked me what an understatement was ! Usually I am delighted to answer my housekeeper's many questions on this and that, but this was an exceptional occasion, so I just said that it was the exact opposite to an *over*statement and left it at that !

I bathed my feet and put on fresh socks. I had a double whiskey from the bottle my friend W. James had given me four months before. I then went to my bedroom and stripped off every bit of clothing and changed into fresh ones. I returned to the kitchen in a warm winter dressing gown. We then had tea, and I untied my parcel of books and examined them. They were a very satisfactory bargain, and I knew where to 'place them'. (In case you are really interested, the E. F. Benson novel went to New York City to nearly complete a Benson collection there. The Strong novel went to Iowa. The magazine with my own work in it went across to Cleveland to a man who collects my writings. The Bradshaw Guide found a home in the Isle of Wight with a man who collects these railway guides. The book on old glass for a very willing buyer in Newcastle-on-Tyne. I made a good profit and delighted five of my clients).

After tea I sat before the fire and thought over the events of the day. The only amusing thing was the faces of the two men in that cafe as they saw me making boots socks out of paper to sop up the wet in my boots. They must have known as I did, that the moment I went outside again the boots would leak in a few minutes. I couldn't think of anything else that was funny and I knew that when I wrote it up in my diary it would appear as a sad experience. I became dozey and longed for my bed.

'Well Lizzie, it's bedtime.' I got up and made for the door. As I was opening it she said, 'Fred, what *is* an *over*statement ?'

'Lizzie, my dear Lizzie, an overstatement is that Fishing is a SPORT. That is an overstatement ! Goodnight !' And off I went to bed, dead tired, and so *ended* Fishing for *me*.

January 1960

For ten years I've had the earnest ambition to spend four weeks in the U S A to give lectures on British books and authors – and Heaven knows that I know my subject. In those ten years I've written six times to the British Council and four times to the English Speaking Union asking if they could in any way help to make this wish come true. All, in various ways, said No. None of them said so, but I bet it's because I lack an old school tie. Isn't 38 years amongst famous authors, listening attentively to their ideals, dreams and methods, long enough ? Isn't four hundred talks in England enough experience for the U S A ? A chap in Texas said that as soon as he'd completed a four million dollar deal he would be sending a plane for me to take me to the U S A as his guest. Alas, for seven months he has been owing me 7 dollars, so I suppose the four million didn't come off. Bang goes my long long ambition, to take tea with Gipsy Rose Lee, buy Jack Dempsey a drink and chat with Hy Gardner.

1960. Who am I anyway ?

Two years ago I was billed (against my wishes) as the Norman Wisdom of the lecture platform. This year I've been called the George Jessel of English after-dinner speakers. When will they let me off these back-handed compliments and let me be just myself ?

My latest after-dinner tale was told in Birmingham. A lady wanted relief from an aid society. She said that her husband had deserted her eight years ago and she had six children. The relief man was just going to make some comment when she said, 'And *don't* you make something of it ! Can I help it if my husband is a perfect gentleman and sometimes comes back home to apologise ?'

1960. It might have been me

I've just seen a film called 'The Beloved Infidel', which is the love story of S. Graham and Scott Fitzgerald. It's of interest – to me at least – to record that in 1927, when I was 20 and she was 21, I was very very much in love with her. I adored her as one does a priceless flower. To think that if I'd made the grade Gregory Peck might have been acting the part of me instead of Fitzgerald.

1960

For ten years my pal Stanley Rubinstein has had locked up a T V game I devised called 'Toe The Line', in which any four men chosen by ballot from a male audience have to come up on the stage and propose to four very beautifull women chosen by the T V company. Each man to have just two minutes, and *not* to touch the girl but to toe the line 2 feet away from her. Best of the 4 by audience applause gets either a kiss from the girl or a dinner date with her.

I feel that the age of romance is dead today. 'Darling I adore you, please marry me' just ain't good enough. I reckon I could *still* make a very good show and keep going for long over two minutes without repeating myself if the delectable Diana Dors was on that stage. Alas, no T V company will take a chance on this very amusing, very visual test of romance in words.

And it's ten years since I suggested the 'Pensioners'

Parade', a monthly programme for old-age pensioners: 5 minutes of advice and help for them, 5 minutes of songs and tales from them, and finally a choir of old folks. No T V station will look at the idea. And I wrote a *very* funny T V play. It started with these words : 'It was half-past three on a Sunday afternoon when my Aunt Ada, who was looking out of the window at the neighbours, turned into a giraffe. . .' I sent it to T V over five years ago. By now Aunt Ada is a *stuffed* giraffe and it was *such* a funny play. Had I written a grim, sordid, blood-curdling Western I'm sure I'd have heard from them in extreemly favourable terms.

Oh well, I suppose this means now that the dream to be in 'Tonight' will *never* come my way. When I had collected exactly 12,000 autographs in forty years I asked 'Tonight' and 'Late Extra' if I was worthy of a couple of minutes in their programmes. Lor ! I wish I hadn't asked ! Oh well, there is always bookselling – till they make talking books, then I will go on the dole in this glorious welfare state where the authorities keep less and less in touch with the workers, and the YOU'S and the NON-YOU'S get further apart.

Agate's last laugh. 23rd February 1960

Yesterday in a parcel of books I'd bought to aid a charity there was a copy of the *Oxford Book of English Verse*, edited by Sir Arthur Quiller-Couch (when I asked for his autograph more than 30 years ago I thought I was asking Sir Arthur Conan Doyle). Now, verse has never been much in my line, but something prompted me to look up and read for the *first* time in my life *The Ancient Mariner* by Coleridge. And I've had quite a SHOCK !

Dear old James Agate, so long after his departure to some land far from ours, has played a neat trick on me and must at this moment be having such a good laugh, for I have been landed with a title for my last book which was given to me long years ago by him ! 'When you want to end your diaries call the last one The Last Bassoon, my boy. It comes from the Ancient Mariner and will suit you down to the ground.' Now, diary, I had a lifelong admiration for Mr Agate and always took what he said for *gospel*. Maybe to some slight degree I even patterned my own life something on his lines. I knew him long before he became famous, and fame at no time changed him for me. Bless his heart, he's had a LAST LAUGH. He must have known that I would take what he said as correct, that The Last Bassoon was in this notable poem, but I find that all that's mentioned is the LOUD bassoon !

I am stuck with a title and can do nothing whatever about it. Well, let him have his last laugh. I do not begrudge it him. He was a kindly old man with his own brand of humour, and this is probally an extreemly good sample of it !

Have I ever been the *loud* Bassoon ? On my oath I don't think so. I've mostly walked *away* from the limelight. I know it has been too much I and not enough Thou, but no one but Lizzie would share my life, and without relations it just *had* to be I, or spend my life in some humdrum manner. And that I didn't want to do, for in my heart I longed to become another Samuel Pepys. Stanley Rubinstein said several times that the mantel of James Agate had most certainly fallen on me. Well, from under its covering I can hear at this moment a chuckle ; it's Jimmy saying, 'I had you, my boy . . . I had you. You *know* I'm a kidder.' Perhaps his kindly interest is watching over me, and *The Last Bassoon* is a better title. We shall see, as the years roll on.

Taking a bow. February 1960

Billy Rose once said that no man carries a chip on his shoulder who is allowed to take a bow. I will take a bow – out of the rat race. When I started writing in 1930 the critics were understanding and kind. Sir Compton Mackenzie, Swinnerton, M. Sadleir, Ivor Brown – these and others gave you a kindly hearing. Nowadays there are only angry young men, who seem to enjoy being cruel. I would be far below their notice, and thank God for that ! But I have had in my time four huge letters of praise from J. Cooper Powys and five from W. de la Mare. I've had three letters of genuine congratulation from Henry Miller. Will today's angry young critics get as good ? I wish them luck. I would not be in their shoes for ten thousand quid. I prefer peace and quiet.

Goodbye. 1st March 1960

I have seemed to get no relief from my fan mail and my hospitality over the past ten years, but for S.A.E. or not I will always answer my mail and offer hospitality to my readers. My At Home day has always been Thursday, for that's early closing day, and there is a little more quiet.

I am ever deeply gratefull to my readers. Over 5,000 wrote asking for MORE when Diary Two was published. Not to have compiled Diary Three would have been proper potty. If as the years go on, say 2,000 ask for another Basonfull then I may return, but I doubt if they will, for my loyal fans are dying and the youngsters of today seek Rock and Roll and I can do neither. All that I've ever been is a very working-class author. I started out from Walworth and the address has remained the same : 152 Westmoreland Road, Walworth, London S.E.17.

I am,

Sincerely,

FRED BASON

Index